INSIGHT POCKET GUIDE

Bangkok

MAR 2024

W9-CHL-051

Discovery
CHANNEL

APA PUBLICATIONS
Part of the Langenscheidt Publishing Group

L

Welcome!

This guidebook combines the interests and enthusiasms of two of the world's best-known information providers: Insight Guides, who have set the standard for visual travel guides since 1970, and Discovery Channel, the world's premier source of non-fiction television programming.

Few cities fire the traveller's imagination with as many exotic images as Bangkok does. Golden temple spires, serpentine canals, monks chanting ancient sutras, classical dancers with fingers bent into impossible angles; these are some of the more evocative images that leap out from postcards of fascinating Krung Thep, the 'City of Angels'. To help you savour this sensory overload, Insight's correspondent to Thailand, Steve Van Beek, has put together a series of itineraries that are perfect for a short stay. Choose from full-day tours that will familiarise you with the main city sights, shorter options that take you from the cacophony of street markets to the tranquility of Buddhist temples, and day excursions further afield to the ancient city of Ayutthaya and the River Kwai. Chapters on eating out, shopping and nightlife, and a useful practical information section complete this reader-friendly guide.

Steve Van Beek – award-winning writer, filmmaker and Insight correspondent – first visited Bangkok some 20 years ago on holiday, but, like many foreigners, he was charmed into staying much longer, eventually making it his home. 'On the surface, Bangkok seems little different from other big cities,' he says, 'but give it time and you will find the city challenging each of your senses, involving you in a way that few cities can.' For Van Beek, Bangkok is chaotic and serene, rowdy and gentle, all at the same time. Yet, it is this element of contradiction that draws him to the city, and which he hopes to share with you in this book.

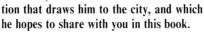

C O N T E N T S

Pages 2/3: A bird's-eye view of Bangkok

Pages 8/9:
The Thai royal family

Why Bangkok Looks Like It Does

It is difficult to picture the city of Bangkok as a riverside fruit orchard. Yet, this was how the city looked 400 years ago: a *bang* (village) of a few thatched houses among the *kok* (wild plum) trees growing along the banks of the Chao Phraya River. About three centuries ago, Bangkok was a duty port for tall ships bearing the cargoes of the world. The ships would stop here for customs inspection on their way to the Thai capital at Ayutthaya, 80km (50 miles) up the river.

By 1650, the town had grown. Among the thatched houses were permanent dwellings occupied by Chinese merchants and court officials who were assigned to monitor river traffic. A pair of French-built, star-shaped fortresses served as sentinels at this gateway to the north. One sat just south of a small Buddhist temple called Wat Po, and the other on the opposite bank in Thonburi, at the mouth of Bangkok Yai canal. Today, the latter's whitewashed, crenellated walls stand as a silent reminder of a former age.

In the 17th century, foreign meddling in its political affairs had forced Thailand to close its doors to all Europeans for 150 years. Missionaries and a few merchants, however, prised Bangkok open in the 1830s, and by 1860, trade and amity treaties had been established with many European countries and North America.

The year 1767 was catastrophic for the Thais. Fabled Ayutthaya, which for 400 years was one of the richest cities in the East, was overrun and torched by the Burmese. The remnants of the Thai army fled south to Thonburi, where they established a temporary capital. It served as a staging area for ceaseless battles with the Burmese, the Laotians and the Vietnamese, all of whom were determined to incorporate Thailand into their own empires.

By 1782, the wars had subsided and a general named Chakri was invited to assume the throne. One of his first decisions was to move the capital across the river to Bangkok, where Chinese merchants had established themselves, and where there was more room for the city to grow. He asked the Chinese merchants to move southeast to the Sampeng area. On the land they vacated, he began the construction of Wat Phra Kaeo, the Temple of the Emerald Buddha, to hold the kingdom's most famous Buddha image, a small jade statue which supposedly provides divine protection to any city that owns it.

War captives were employed to dig a defensive moat across a river bend to make the royal city an island. Two more moats were dug in concentric arcs to the east. King Rama I, the dynastic name General Chakri chose for himself, understood the value of symbolism in rebuilding his people's shattered confidence. He strove not simply to establish a capital, but to create a new Ayutthaya with symbols evoking its grandeur and glory. The royal name for the city included the designation *Krung Thep*, or 'City of Angels', by which Ayutthaya had been known. It is the name Thais call Bangkok today.

To establish more tangible links with Ayutthaya, King Rama I dismantled the walls of the ruined city. He transported Ayutthayan bricks downriver on barges to Bangkok and incorporated them into a stout wall running along the banks of the river and the second canal, to surround the city and complete its defenses. In similar fashion, Rama I transported famous Buddha images from old Thai cities and installed them in Bangkok's new temples. At his death in 1809, Bangkok was a thriving city well on its way to reclaiming its former prominence in Asia.

The two kings credited with modernising Thailand were King Mongkut (1851–1868) and his son King Chulalongkorn (1868–1910). King Mongkut, a remarkable man unfortunately lampooned in the musical *The King and I*, built the city's first paved street, Charoen Krung (New Road), in 1863. Chulalongkorn continued the modernisation process, building a rail line north, adding more city roads and constructing a tram line. It was during his reign that most of the grand European-style buildings were constructed: the Defence Ministry, Vimarnmek and many of the buildings along outer Ratchadamnoen Avenue. Elsewhere, the Thais built the three-storey shop houses that hem most city streets today.

As Bangkok moved into the 20th century, it began growing east and northwards. Silom (Windmill) Road changed from a rural area of cattle markets, rice fields and market gardens into a residential area. The eastern boundary of the city was the railroad track at the

An early Bangkok scene: negotiating the canals

end of Ploenchit Road, but the areas in between started to fill with houses and shops. In 1932, the Memorial Bridge, the city's first bridge, was built. It linked Bangkok and Thonburi and spurred development on the western side of the river, which was previously covered by jungle. By the 1950s, most of the canals had been filled in, and citizens no longer travelled by boats but by cars.

The city's big construction boom came in the 1960s during the Vietnam War, when vast amounts of money poured into Thailand. The first multi-storey office buildings were erected, and Sukhumvit Road, once a country lane, became a concrete canyon. The two-lane road that led to Don Muang Airport, deep in the countryside, was widened to four lanes and then, in the 1970s, to 10 lanes. With the modernisation came many of the traffic, communications and pollution problems that plague Bangkok today.

The 1990s are witness to the most dramatic transformation in the city's history, with the skyline changing almost weekly. A village of a few dozen people has burgeoned into a throbbing city of around eight million people. Aside from Chinatown, which has retained much of its cultural identity, most of the ethnic sections of the city have become homogenised. Bangkok has come to look more and more like modern cities everywhere in the world.

Landmarks

Bangkok is a confusing city for the visitor. It is flat and without natural landmarks and it lacks a distinctive city centre. Roads run in all directions and a street can change its name four times along its length. There are, however, some discernible sections. The area around the Temple of the Emerald Buddha holds most of the city's antique architecture. Most of the government ministries are found in this area and also along Ratchadamnoen Avenue. Chinatown lies between Charoen Krung and the river. The city's business section (if one can be said to exist) occupies the area between Siphya and Sathorn roads and between Rama IV Road and Charoen Krung.

Most of the hotels lie east of Phya Thai Road and south of the Victory Monument. The major shopping areas are along Rama 1, Ploenchit, Ratchadamri, Silom and Suriwong roads.

Bangkok rush-hour traffic

Saffron-robed monks are found everywhere

The Angels of Krung Thep

What infuses Bangkok's bland concrete enclaves with personality are its people. The Thais' graciousness and charm give a vital dimension to a visit; often it is their smiles that are indelibly imprinted on a visitor's memory long after he returns home. Who are these people and where did they come from? Discounting the prehistoric tribes who mysteriously disappeared, it is thought that the Thais originated in China and moved south from the 10th century on. Whatever their origins, Thai blood was augmented by infusions of Vietnamese, Cambodian, Laotian, Mon Burmese, Malay, Japanese, Indian and even Persian strains, whose features are visible in many faces today.

The most prominent ethnic group, the Chinese, have managed to retain much of their original culture. But even these people have been rapidly absorbed into the Thai fabric. The smooth integration into society has meant that Thailand is rare among Asian countries in having avoided class, ethnic, religious, or civil wars. The strong Thai sense of self and independence also helped it to avoid colonisation by foreign powers.

Thai tranquillity comes from a supreme tolerance of others. This stems in large part from the practice of Hinayana Buddhism, which 92 percent of the nation professes. Buddhism teaches a doctrine of acceptance of the vagaries of life. This, coupled with a strong belief in *sanuk*, or 'fun', gives Thais a sense of *joie de vivre*. It may sound trite, but look at a group of Thais and invariably you will see them laughing together.

At some point, almost every Buddhist man spends at least a week, or more, as a monk. In the monastery, he learns the tenets of his religion and meditates on ways of improving himself. By ancient tradition, women cannot be ordained as

Buddhism

Prince Siddartha was born in Lumpini, southern Nepal, in 543 BC. He lived a life of luxury, marrying a princess and fathering a child. It was only as an adult that he ventured beyond the palace walls where he saw a poor man, a sick man and a dead man. Disturbed by this suffering, he left his life of luxury to become an ascetic.

Deciding that fasting was not the path to salvation, he began meditating. While trying to reach enlightenment, he was tempted by demons, an event called *The Battle with Mara* that is normally depicted on the inner back walls of wats. He preached a doctrine of moderation, choosing the Middle Way over extremes as a means of eliminating personal suffering.

His life and final incarnations before being born as the Buddha are normally depicted on the side and back interior walls of temples. In addition to Buddhist religious holidays, there is a weekly *wan phra*, a holy day whose date is determined by the lunar calendar. In the morning, you can hear the monks praying the ancient chants.

Thai men are expected to spend part of their lives as monks

monks (although some women shave their heads and don white robes to become lay nuns). Thus, a monk makes merit not only for himself, but for his mother and his sisters, thus ensuring that they will be re-born into a higher plane of existence in their next life.

Buddhist tolerance extends to the other faiths. Mosques, Chinese Mahayana Buddhist temples, Christian churches, and Sikh and Hindu temples stand side by side with Buddhist *wat* (temples). These are testament to the open worship of all religions, a freedom granted not just by the constitution, but accepted as a fact of life.

Beneath the faith in Buddhism is an older belief in animism. Trees and other objects are thought to contain spirits which must be placated to avoid bringing harm to oneself. Thus, every home and office building has a spirit house in its compound where the rampant spirits of the dead or of trees felled to construct the building can reside. Thais take these beliefs very seriously, placing incense and flowers on the shrine each morning or evening.

In contrast to Buddhist monks are long-haired, white-robed Brahman priests, who are responsible for royal rites of passage and officiate at royal ceremonies of state. They are seen in public only on rare occasions, such as for the annual Ploughing Ceremony.

To the cornerstones of a fervent belief in the nation and in religion is added a third which binds all Thais together: reverence for the monarchy. This is not a blind worship of royalty but a genuine admiration for the current king and his family, who have earned respect by devotion to their subjects. The present monarch, King Bhumibol Adulyadej, who celebrated his 50th year on the throne in 1996, has spent a considerable amount of time in the countryside working with farmers on rural development projects. The portraits of King Bhumibol and Queen Sirikit, which hang in homes and offices, are not hung up out of habit but out of genuine respect.

Whatever your thoughts about monarchy in the modern world, keep them to yourself, as insults to the royal family are the one area where the Thais show little tolerance. Since 1932, Thailand has been governed as a constitutional monarchy, although the king exercises more moral suasion than political power.

Historical Highlights

3,500 BC: Bronze Age culture created by an unknown people thrives at Ban Chieng in northeast Thailand.

8th–12th century: The Thais migrate from China into northern Thailand, which is controlled by the Khmer empire administered from Cambodia.

1238: Khmer power wanes, and the Thais, led by King Intradit, establish an independent nation based at Sukhothai.

1350: Ayutthaya, farther south on the Chao Phraya River, supplants Sukhothai as Thailand's capital.

1767: After repeated attempts, Burmese armies succeed in overrunning Ayutthaya, stripping it of its population and treasures and destroying the city. The Thai army regroups at Thonburi and engages in 15 years of wars with the Burmese, Laotians and Vietnamese.

1782: The wars subside. General Chakri assumes the throne. Taking the name of Rama I, he establishes the Chakri dynasty, of which the present king is the ninth monarch. Rama I moves his capital across the river to Bangkok.

1851: King Mongkut, the monarch depicted in *The King and I*, ascends the throne after 27 years as a Buddhist monk. He reforms the laws and sets Thailand on the path towards modernisation. He encourages contact with the West, signing a treaty with Britain in 1855.

1868–1910: King Chulalongkorn, one of history's most dynamic kings, continues his father's initiatives and Thailand moves firmly into the 20th century. By political manoeuvring, he preserves the sovereignty of Thailand, the only Southeast Asian nation that escapes colonisation.

1911–25: King Vajiravudh concentrates on political reforms, giving greater freedom and encouraging criticism of government policies. Thailand sides with the Allies during World War I.

1926–35: Economic troubles stemming from the Depression years compound King Prajadhipok's problems, and in 1932, a revolution occurs which replaces absolute monarchy with constitutional monarchy.

1936–46: Ananda Mahidol, is named king but returns to Switzerland to complete his studies. Thailand is occupied by the Japanese during the war. In 1946, King Ananda dies and is succeded by his younger brother, Bhumibol Adulyadej.

1950–72: On 5 May, Prince Bhumibol is crowned King. The 50s are times of turmoil for Thailand, with many coups d'etat and a succession of military-backed governments. In the 1960s, Thailand experiences an economic boom as a result of investment by the US.

1973–90: A popular uprising topples a despised dictatorship, ushering in a three-year period of true democracy. However, a right-wing counter-coup in 1976 re-establishes military rule. Several governments are chosen in popular elections.

1991: Public reaction over a military coup d'etat against a supposedly corrupt government results in the appointment of former diplomat Anand Panyarachun as Prime Minister. His government is one of the most able and popular in 50 years.

1992: In May, public demand for a return to democracy leads to an army massacre that leaves hundreds dead. In September, elections are held and a new government formed.

1995: Leading opposition party Chart Thai is surprisingly elected to power with Barnharn Silpa-archa as Prime Minister.

1996: Thailand celebrates 50 years of King Bhumibol's monarchy.

1997: Thailand enters a recession. A new government under Prime Minister Chuan Leekpai, leader of the Democrat Party is elected.

1998–9: Thailand follows guidelines set by the International Monetary Fund to help revive the economy.

Thai Culture

What distinguishes Bangkok from other large Asian capitals is the wealth of traditional architecture and art it holds. Everything that one associates with the exotic Orient – fabulous palaces, glittering temples, beautiful Buddha images and ornate art – is found here, and in great abundance. Better still, much of the art is transportable, which makes shopping a prime reason for a visit.

Although having many antecedents, Thai art has a style which is unique. Nothing can compare in design or execution with the Temple of the Emerald Buddha and the Grand Palace (see *Day 2, page 24*). Despite the fact that the temples and *stupas* found throughout the city and the countryside display differences that reflect varying influences and periods in Thai art history, they are instantly recognisable as Thai.

Thailand has also produced a wide range of applied arts, mostly for the purpose of beautifying temples. Mother-of-pearl was developed to decorate temple doors and royal utensils. Black and gold lacquer scenes cover temple doors and windows, and the cabinets that hold religious manuscripts. Murals on the inner walls of the temples tell the story of Buddha's life or of his last incarnations before he was born as the Buddha. Images of Buddha have been carved from stone and wood, cast from bronze, and shaped from clay in various styles and forms.

Silversmithing, goldsmithing, jewellery and nielloware beautify utensils used in royal ceremonies. Because the Thais cannot resist decorating even the most mundane utensils, village crafts like basketry, silk and cotton weaving, and pottery are elevated to an art form, resulting in objects that are beautiful as they are practical.

Theatre and dance has been the principal mode of transmitting ancient stories. The most important source for theatrical productions has been the *Ramakien*. This Thai version of an Indian classical tale, *The Ramayana*, tells the story of the abduction of the beautiful Sita, wife of the god-king Phra Ram, by the treacherous demon king Tosakan. The story is usually depicted by huge leather shadow puppets, actors, masked actors and puppets.

Thai dance is often rooted in ancient mythology

Values

Sanuk is a concept loosely translated as 'fun'. Thais judge the value of an endeavour by the amount of *sanuk* it contains; anything not *sanuk* is to be avoided. Another Thai attitude worth understanding is that of *mai pen rai*, which is related to the Buddhist ideal of avoiding suffering. *Mai pen rai* is translated variously as 'it doesn't matter' or 'no problem', and is usually accompanied by a shrug of the shoulders. The surprise is that despite this attitude, Thais are dynamic, as Bangkok's rapid development amply demonstrates.

Women enjoy a degree of freedom not found in many countries. While many women in the lower economic groups have not yet obtained the protection from exploitation guaranteed by the constitution, those in the upper echelons have gained a degree of power envied by women elsewhere. It's not unusual to see major international companies headed by Thai women.

Although Thailand has had to struggle to maintain its values in the face of the onslaught of materialism, it has managed to acquire an equilibrium that is admirable. These traits – equanimity, warmth and a gentle culture – have drawn visitors for centuries, enveloping them in their warm embrace.

Wat Etiquette

Wat, or temples, are open to all visitors. Of all the *wat* in Bangkok, only the Temple of the Emerald Buddha (Wat Phra Kaeo), Wat Po, Wat Benchamabophit and Wat Arun charge admission fees to cover restoration costs. Admission to the rest is free.

It is worth remembering a few things when visiting temples. Disrespect towards Buddha images, temples or monks is not taken lightly. Take off your shoes before entering a *wat*, and make sure you are appropriately attired: long pants are acceptable but not shorts. Monks observe strict vows of chastity that prohibit their being touched by women, even their mothers. Do not climb on *stupas* or treat Buddha images disrespectfully. You may photograph monks, *wat*, images (except for the Emerald Buddha) and all Buddhist ceremonies.

Paying homage at the Erawan Shrine

Bangkok

400 m / 440 yards

Bangkok's haphazard growth over the past few centuries presents a challenge for visitors finding their way around. Lacking a grid system, Bangkok's streets can have as many as four different names along their lengths. There is no distinct business district, nor are there any easily identifiable landmarks. Often, shops, restaurants and houses don't display street numbers. While the heat, humidity and traffic congestion all conspire against making this a city for walkers, those who persevere will be amply rewarded by the sights and sounds of an Asian metropolis.

Never mind if you get lost or stray from the suggested itineraries: there are numerous lanes and alleys into which you can wander to discover Bangkok's secrets (and umpteen coffeeshops when you need an icy-cold drink). Although few Thais speak English, they are ever willing to help lost visitors. If you stop a Thai and ask for directions, chances are he or she will walk you to your destination. Other than the occasional purse snatcher or pickpocket, street crime against travellers is rare, even in darkened alleys at night.

The first three Day Itineraries are designed to capture the flavour of the city. These are followed by a series of half-day itineraries – some best done in the mornings and others in the afternoons – which explore interesting aspects of the city in greater detail. Finally, a selection of excursions take you out of the city limits to explore greater Bangkok. Although several of the itineraries involve some walking, you can easily hop onto a *tuk-tuk* (three-wheeled, open-air taxi) or a motorcycle taxi to cover longer distances.

Since *Day 1* starts early in the morning, make sure you've spent some time beforehand relaxing and getting used to the climate. An afternoon in the hotel pool should do the trick. Arm yourself with a bottle of drinking water and an umbrella if you're there during the rainy season from June to October, and you're ready to discover the enigma that is Bangkok.

DAY 1

Getting Acquainted

A walk and breakfast in Lumpini Park; Erawan Shrine; an Oriental bazaar; a sky-high lunch; crafts browsing; a flower market; down river on an express boat; and an atmospheric tea at the Oriental, followed by a Thai-style dinner and culture show.

This itinerary is designed to expose you to as many sensations as possible. It will also orient you so that you can find your way around the city. Begin at 7am with a walk in **Lumpini Park** (Suan Loom). Lumpini is a magnet for joggers, workers grabbing steaming bowls of noodles on their way to work, health-minded Chinese doing their *tai chi* exercises, and Chinese swordsmen practising ancient rituals with silver broadswords. On Sunday, rent a boat and paddle near the island, where you will see a group of Chinese playing traditional instruments.

When you have seen enough, head for the northwest corner of the park to **Pop Restaurant** for an American or Thai breakfast under the trees. After breakfast, leave Pop Restaurant to the right, exiting the west gate onto Ratchadamri Road. It is a 1-km (½-mile) walk to the right along Ratchadamri to the Rama I intersection

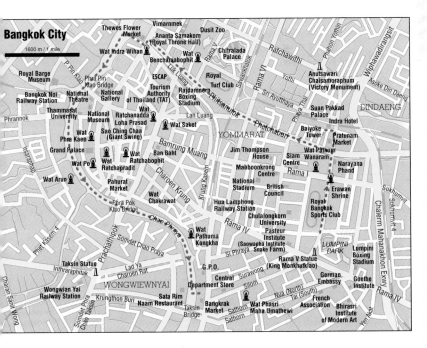

Pavement vendors at the Pratunam market

so cross the street and catch a bus (any route number will do), a taxi, or *tuk-tuk*. Alight just before the busy Rama I intersection and cross to the Grand Hyatt Erawan Hotel with its ornate soaring columns. On the corner is the **Erawan Shrine** (late risers may wish to have breakfast at the Grand Hyatt and begin this itinerary at the Erawan Shrine at about 9am). The shrine is well-known for granting wishes for success in love, examinations and the lottery. You may also wish to ask for blessings by buying incense, candles and flowers and uttering a short prayer for good luck.

Exit the Erawan Shrine, angle right and cross Ploenchit Road. Continue along Ratchadamri Road, noting the location of the **Narayana Phand** (open daily 10am–8pm) shopping mall at 127 Ratchadamri Road, guarded by two *yaksa* (giant demons). You will return here after lunch. Continue along Ratchadamri, cross the canal and the intersection where Ratchadamri runs beneath an overpass and changes its name to Ratchaprarop. You are now in a real Thai market called **Pratunam**. Begin by looking at the displays of the pavement vendors. When you see a lane running east between the buildings, follow it into the market, which lies behind the building facades. Here, you will find fresh produce and household items that the Thais use in their daily lives. Walk through it to see what life in old Bangkok was before the advent of supermarkets.

Continue on Ratchaprarop to the pedestrian bridge and cross to the Indra Hotel. Just behind is one of Bangkok's somewhat taller buildings, **Baiyoke Suite Hotel**, painted in a rainbow of colours. Ride the elevator to the 4th floor and change to the elevator in the inner lobby which takes you to the **Sky Lounge** (daily, 11–2am) restaurant on the 77th floor. With a magnificent panoramic view of the city, Sky Lounge serves Thai, Chinese and European food for lunch. Get out your pull-out map and try to identify the city landmarks. Before leaving, call the Oriental Hotel's **Sala Rim Naam** restaurant (tel: 2360400) for dinner reservations at 7pm.

After lunch, return to the **Narayana Phand** mall, which you had

22

passed earlier, along Ratchadamri Road. This is the government's handicraft store. Wander through it for a good idea of the variety and quality of crafts available in Thailand. If nothing else, it is a mini-museum of Thailand's crafts.

At about 3.30pm, exit Narayana Phand and turn left to cross the pedestrian overpass to the looming World Trade Center. Here, hail a taxi and ask the driver to take you to the **Thewes** (Ta-laat Tay-wait) **Flower Market**. It sells both cut flowers and potted plants and provides a good introduction to the flora of tropical Asia. If you are running late and the sun is getting to you, skip the market. Walk along the canal to the river. At the boat landing, buy a dock ticket and wait for the express boat (*rua duan*) travelling downriver from right to left. The boat is long, narrow and painted white with a red trim. Tell the conductor you want to go to the Oriental Hotel and pay the requisite fare.

The express boat is one of Asia's great travel bargains, a breezy way to see the city's principal monuments. On the left before the bridge is one of the two remaining watchtowers of the city wall. Beyond the bridge on the left is **Thammasat University** with its conical watchtower. You then have a beautiful view of the **Grand Palace** and, on the right, **Wat Arun**, the Temple of Dawn. On your left past the next bridge is the rear of Chinatown. Shortly thereafter comes the Hotel Sofitel, the Royal Orchid Sheraton Hotel, the Portuguese Embassy, the French Embassy and the **Oriental Hotel**. Get off at the Oriental Hotel landing and make your way to the hotel.

This is one of the classic hotels of Asia and its **Author's Lounge** is one of the reasons why. Order tea and relax for a while under the bamboo trees. Stay here until sunset or walk through the Oriental Plaza just behind the hotel where you can shop for gift items. At about 6.45pm, walk through the Oriental's lobby to the private boat landing. The boat that ferries diners to the **Sala Rim Naam** restaurant across the river is free. Enjoy a delicious Thai dinner followed by a programme of Thai classical dancing.

Sip on a gin tonic at the Oriental's Verandah Terrace as dusk falls

DAY 2

Breakfast on the river bank and boat upriver to the Temple of the Emerald Buddha (Wat Phra Kaeo) and the Grand Palace.

Begin the day with a buffet breakfast on the edge of the river. The Shangri-La Hotel's **Coffee Garden** and the Oriental's **Verandah Terrace** are both excellent and highly recommended. About 9am, walk to the boat landing at the end of Soi Oriental (on the south side of the Oriental hotel). There, board an express boat heading upriver to your right. Disembark at **Tha Chang Wang Luang** landing just past the Grand Palace, visible on your right. Walk straight down the street about 200m (218yds) to the entrance of the **Temple of the Emerald Buddha** and the **Grand Palace** (both open daily 8.30am–3.30pm) which stands on the right behind a tall, white stucco wall. Make sure you are dressed decently, ie no shorts, as inappropriately dressed visitors have been known to be refused admission.

No matter how much you've heard or how many photographs you've seen of the Grand Palace and the Temple of the Emerald Buddha, also known as Wat Phra Kaeo, you can never be quite prepared for the glittering reality of these suburb buildings. The admission ticket admits you to both the aforementioned buildings, the Wat Phra Kaeo Museum, the Coins and Decorations Museum

The Grand Palace roofline – skyward bound

in the same vicinity, and Vimarnmek (see *Pick and Mix 1*) across town. Just before entering Wat Phra Kaeo, note the entrance to the Coins and Decorations Museum on your right because you will return here later. Save the museum for last, not because it is the least important part of the tour but because it is air-conditioned and you will want to get most of the walking out of the way before the midday sun fries you.

Bronzed kinara

Unlike the rest of Bangkok's 28,000 *wat*, no monks live in Wat Phra Kaeo. The first major architectural complex built in Bangkok, its principal building, the **Chapel Royal**, was constructed in 1784 to house the kingdom's most sacred **Emerald Buddha** image. It was reputedly found in Chiang Rai in the early 1400s and is claimed to bestow good fortune on the kingdom that possesses it. Sitting high on a pedestal, protected by a nine-tiered umbrella and flanked by crystal balls representing the sun and the moon, the 75-cm (30-in) high jadeite image surprises many visitors by its small size. That it is venerated in such a lavish manner leaves no doubt about its importance to the Thais. Three times a year, at the beginning of each new season, the king presides over the changing of the Emerald Buddha's robes: a golden, diamond-studded tunic for the hot season, a gilded robe flecked with blue for the rainy season, and a robe of enamel-coated solid gold for the cool season.

Among the other buildings guarded by the *yaksa* (giant demons) are the trio of structures to the right of the Chapel Royal. The one on the east is the **Prasad Phra Tepidon** or Royal Pantheon, which holds the statues of the first eight Chakri kings. It is ringed by gilded bronze *kinara* and *kinaree*, graceful half-human, half-bird figures. To the west, the **Library** holds the *Tripataka*, the holy Buddhist scriptures. The tallest structure is the huge gilded **Phra Si Rattana Jedi**, covered in gold mosaic tiles. Just north of these monuments is a model of **Angkor Wat**, the great holy city of the Khmer empire in the 11th and 12th century. The walls of the cloisters around the complex are covered in murals recounting the *Ramakien* story. Look in the outer areas of each scene for charming depictions of daily life and traditional entertainments.

From Wat Phra Kaeo, walk south into the compound containing the **Grand Palace**. Since 1946, the Thai royal family has lived in Chitrlada Palace in the northern area of Bangkok but the Grand Palace is still used for state ceremonies. The first building is the **Amarin Vinitchai Throne**. It served as royal residences for the first three Rama kings. In the first hall is the boat-shaped throne before which legal cases requiring royal adjudication were heard. Behind it was Rama I's bedchamber. Since his reign, each new monarch has slept in it the first night after his coronation. In the courtyard are gold-knobbed red poles where the royal elephants were once tethered.

Wat Phra Kaeo bathed by the evening light

The centrepiece is the majestic **Chakri Maha Prasad** with its three spires atop an Italian Renaissance-style building. Constructed in 1882, it was the last building to be erected in the Grand Palace. Wander through the state drawings rooms, decorated in the manner of European palaces with some very Thai touches to maintain the perspective. To the west is the **Dusit Maha Prasad**, or Audience Hall, where kings once conducted state businesses. It is now the final resting place for deceased kings before they are cremated in the nearby Sanam Luang field.

To the northwest is the **Wat Phra Kaeo Museum**, which contains a collection of beautiful Buddha images made of crystal, silver, ivory and gold as well as some beautiful lacquer screens. In the southern room on the second floor are two very interesting scale models of the Grand Palace/Wat Phra Kaeo complex; one as it looked over 100 years ago and the other as it looks today.

Exit the museum and angle to the right to a restaurant with an open verandah. Here, you can enjoy a panoramic view of the Dusit Maha Prasad. Order a chilled coconut. Drink the clear, sweet liquid through a straw and scrape out the tender white flesh with a spoon. The shop also sells Chiang Mai paper umbrellas, handy for warding off the sun, the rain, and pesky souvenir salesmen.

Afterwards, exit the Grand Palace and walk past the ticket booth to the **Coins and Decorations Museum** (open daily 9am–3.30pm). Downstairs are ceramic coins, silver bullet money, seals and money from the other regions of Thailand and the world. Upstairs are beautiful royal crowns, jewelled swords, jewellery, medals, brocaded robes, and betelnut sets which signify one's royal rank.

It has been a hot, hard morning so the afternoon is yours to shop, swim, or just relax. Dine at **The Tycoon**, 118/29-32 Sukhumvit Soi 23. Its international menu, tasteful piano bar offerings and classical Asian sculpture and ceramics provide a memorable experience.

DAY ③

Damnern Saduak Floating Market and the Rose Garden

By boat through the Damnern Saduak Floating Market, the world's tallest Buddhist stupa, and a cultural show at the Rose Garden.

Over the years, the popular **Damnern Saduak Floating Market** has outgrown several sites and moved farther into the countryside of Ratchaburi Province, 110km (70miles) west of Bangkok. Still, it has lost little of its appeal. Because of the distance involved, one may be tempted to book a guided tour. Nearly every agency offers the same package and for about the same price – less than 1,000 baht – which includes an air-conditioned bus ride, lunch and all entrance fees. Be prepared to contend with the crowds: by the time your tour bus arrives, so will have all the others.

The tour begins around 7am with a pick-up from your hotel. The early start is to give you a jump both on the traffic and the early-rising vendors who begin paddling towards the market well before dawn. You drive through the Thonburi countryside, stopping to photograph the **Samut Sakhon salt flats**. Its windmills draw sea water for evaporation into table salt. At a boat landing, you board a long-tailed boat for a fast, exhilarating ride through the canals to the Damnern Saduak Floating Market. There are actually three concentrated areas of floating markets. Most tours stop at **Talaat Hia Kui**, a parallel canal to Damnern Saduak. Souvenir shops are aplenty in this area.

The floating market is an Asian wonder unique to Thailand, not merely on Damnern Saduak, which functions as a legitimate market and not one merely staged for tourists, but also in the hundreds of lush lowland canals and rivers throughout Thailand. Village

Bartering across water at Damnern Saduak

Damnern Saduak is a veritable feast for the senses

women in their dark blue peasant's shirts and colourful *sarong* paddle *sampan* filled with fruits, spices, flowers, sweets and vegetables to trade either with buyers on land or with each other.

On some tours, the next stop is a snake farm, where the normally docile snakes are roused to action by handlers who virtually beat them. If this offends you, be assured that this theatrical demonstration is not the normal practice at authentic snake farms. See the genuine show in Bangkok at the Snake Farm (see *Itinerary 15)*, where snakes are bred for practical and medical purposes, not commercial gain.

The next stop is the town of **Nakhon Pathom** to see the colossal **Phra Pathom Chedi,** claimed to be the world's tallest Buddhist *stupa*. Originally dating to 300 BC, the *chedi* was raised to its present height of 130m (420ft) by King Mongkut in 1860. Buy incense, a candle and a lotus bud and make a wish. Walk around the *chedi*, which rests on a circular base planted with frangipani trees.

Some 30km (20 miles) to Bangkok is the much-visited **Rose Garden** on the banks of the Ta Chin River. After an included lunch of Thai food, you will be taken to its Thai Village for an instant and predictable cultural show. Here, you will see a selection of everything considered typical of the culture of the country: folk dancing, Thai boxing, cockfighting, sword fighting, a wedding and a monk's ordination ceremony. This is followed by a demonstration of elephants at work and the chance to ride on an elephant for a small fee. Finally comes the long ride home through rush-hour traffic, arriving in Bangkok about 7pm. Although the places mentioned in this tour are inundated with tourists, this tour comes highly recommended.

If you don't feel the need to seek refuge in your hotel room, head for an afternoon drink at either the **Siam Inter-Continental** or the **Hilton** hotels: both have beautiful tropical gardens and exotic drinks. Otherwise, go to one of the riverside Thai restaurants listed in the *Eating Out* section of this guide. The adventurous may dine at the stalls along **Taniya Road** (off the upper end of Silom Road) serving noodles and other Thai dishes. One is then within striking distance of the infamous Patpong Road, where varied and often blatantly sexual nightlife abounds.

Right, Phra Pathom Chedi

Morning Itineraries

1. Wat Benchamabophit, Vimarnmek Palace and Dusit Zoo

Rise at dawn to see monks receiving alms at Wat Benchamabophit, on to Dusit Zoo to see exotic animals, and Vimarnmek Palace for royal regalia. Late risers can skip the alms-giving ritual.

Each morning before drawn, some 100,000 Buddhist monks throughout Thailand don their saffron robes and walk through village and city streets. Buddhist families waiting outside their homes place in the monks' *baht* (alms bowls) rice and curries, which they will later eat at their monasteries. This dignified rite provides the monks with their only source of food, gives the laity an opportunity to gain merit to ensure reincarnation as higher beings, and welds the nation into its common Buddhist faith.

At about 6.30am, head by taxi to **Wat Benchamabophit**, the Marble Wat (open daily 8am–5pm), where the arms-giving ritual is slightly altered. Here, the faithful take the food to the monks waiting silently in the tree-shaded street in front of the temple. The alms-giving continues until 7.30am. Proceed through the gate.

Wat Benchamabophit was built in 1911. Sponsored by King Rama V, this was the last major temple constructed in Bangkok. Conceived by the architect Prince Naris, half-brother of the king, the temple is designed in a cruciform shape. The temple exterior is completely clad in Carrara marble from Italy, hence the sobriquet, the

Marble Temple. Inside the temple, colourful stained-glass window depicting angels are a radical departure from traditional Thai window treatments. The Buddha image is an excellent copy of the Phra Buddha Jinnarat, which is found in Phitsanuloke. This statue is said to have wept tears of blood when Ayutthaya overran the northern town of Sukhothai in the 14th century.

In the cloisters behind the *bot* (ordination hall), King Chulalongkorn placed 53 important **Buddha images** – originals and copies – to show his subjects the different ways in which the Buddha had been portrayed throughout history in South and

Italian Carrara marble clads the exterior of Wat Benchamabophit

Southeast Asia. Walk down the aisle, reading the interesting labels at the base of the images. Of special interest is the unusual Walking Buddha from the Sukhothai period.

Walk south across one of the canal bridges – filled with fat catfish – towards a colonial school and into the warren of lanes lined by two-storey houses. These are the *guti,* the monks' homes.

Recross the bridge and exit the *wat* through the northern door onto Sri Ayutthaya Road. Walk left to the next intersection. Turn right into the broad plaza with an equestrian statue of King Chulalongkorn. Walk past it to the imposing white building with a European-style dome. This is the **Atana Samakom Throne Hall**, the former home of Parliament which, unfortunately, is not open to the public. Walk around it to the right.

Halfway around is the gate to **Dusit Zoo** (open daily 8am–6pm). This is Bangkok's only zoo, and although the animals are kept in less than pristine conditions, it does provide a good introduction to

Dusit Zoo

the animals of Asia's jungles, including the royal white elephants, which once determined the magnitude of royal power.

About 10am, or whenever you have seen enough, return to the zoo entrance and continue in the direction you were going before. Behind the Atana Samakom Throne Hall is a gate marked with a fancy sign, **Abhisek Dusit Throne Hall and Support Museum** (open daily 9.30am–4pm; last ticket sold at 3pm). At the entrance, present the ticket you bought at the Grand Palace (see *Day 2*) or pay the requisite entrance fee. Across the well-manicured grounds is a single-storey teak building, the Abhisek Dusit Throne Hall, which houses exquisite Thai handicrafts created by the Queen Sirikit-sponsored SUPPORT Foundation. This is a good introduction to high-quality traditional crafts and arts.

Behind is the **Vimarnmek Palace**. This is the back way to the palace; the palace street entrance is down the road past the first gate you entered. On a hot day, the considerably closer back entrance will be appreciated. Free 45-minute guided English-language tours are conducted at half-hour intervals from 9.30am to 2.45pm. You are not allowed to wander on your own. A free cultural show of traditional Thai dances takes place daily at 10.30am and 2pm.

Vimarnmek (Celestial Residence) was built by King Chulalongkorn as a summer alternative to the more formal Grand Palace. The 100-room house – claimed to be the largest structure in the world made completely of golden teak – and the gardens alone would merit a visit, but it is the art collections that make it especially interesting. Beautifully-crafted dining sets as well as artefacts of the past century imported from Europe testify to superb royal taste.

The Vimarnmek Palace offers a peek into the royal past

Sunrise from the Memorial Bridge; Phak Khlong Talad, the city's fresh produce market; a Thai coffee and Chinese pastry breakfast; the flower market; across the river to Wat Arun; and back to Wat Po for a wander and a Thai massage.

Sunrise over the city skyline and the river is experienced no place better than the **Memorial Bridge** (Saphan Phut). The sun rises about 6.30am, a good half hour before the traffic begins to thicken. Tell the taxi driver to let you off at the foot of the bridge. Climb the stairs and walk to the middle of the new span for a view down-river; then climb to the old span for a view of Wat Arun and the boats upriver. If you are lucky, you may be able to see a few early morning fishermen casting lines from the parapet.

Walk down the stairs and up-river to **Phak Khlong Talad** market (open 24 hours a day). This is the receiving point for fresh flowers, fruits and vegetables brought by long boat from Thonburi's market gardens and sent to the kitchens of Bangkok's hotels and homes. Wander around to see the wide variety of tropical produce on sale.

To leave, walk straight along the road on which you entered the market until you reach an entryway on the right leading into a covered market. From the door, you can see a shrine at the far end with a statue of Rama I, Bangkok's founder. Walk past it, passing sundry and fabric shops until you intersect with busy **Chakkaphet Road**. Turn right past a fish and a goldsmith shop, crossing at the second intersection to a watch shop. In front of it is a one-table pavement coffee shop. Ignore the dust and order Thai coffee, a strong brew made of coffee and chicory beans, and some *patongkoh*, delicious breakfast pastries the Chinese eat with their morning coffee. It's a memorable way to start the day.

Afterwards, cross Chakkaphet Road to the flower vendors whose roses, orchids and other blooms fill the pavements. On a sunny morning, there are fewer pretty sights. Buy a *puang malai* and carry it with you. A few sniffs from time to time will act as a

Wat Arun and Wat Po

400 m / 440 yards

Maharaj Anulet Market · Wat Mahathat & Market · Silpakorn University · SANAM LUANG · Mae Thorani Statue · Astrologers · Sarn Lak Muang · San Chao Pho Sua (Chin. Temple) · City Hall · Wat Ratchanadda · Loha Prasad · Amulet Market · Wat Ratnatdaram · Na Phra Lan · Wat Phra Kaeo · Sanam Chai · Kanlaya Namit · Bamrung · Sao Ching Chaa (Giant Swing) · Muang · Chao Phraya · Grand Palace · Wat Rachapradit · Saran Rom · Khlong Lot · Wat Rachabophit · Dinso · Wat Suthat · Maha Chai · Boriphat · Thai Wang · Wat Po · Phra Phitak · Ti Tong · Charoen Krung · Reclining Buddha · Tha Tien · Sanam Chai · Mehteru · Phahurat · Tri Phet · Pahurat Market · Yaowarat · Phra Pok · Chakkrawat · Ratchawong · Wat Arun (Temple of Dawn) · Café Thai · Chakkaphet · Vegetable & Flower Market · Phak Klong Talad Market · Phra Buddha Yodfa Bridge · Klao Bridge

restorative as you walk through the pall of exhaust smoke towards the boat dock and river-taxi stop called Tha Tien.

Recross Chakkaphet to the coffee shop. Turn right and head up Chakkaphet, which crosses a canal where it changes its name to Maharat and begins to curve to the right. Follow Maharat to the intersection with a street that runs between the Grand Palace and Wat Po. (The sign on the opposite side says 'Soi Thai Wang'.) Turn left and walk to the **Tha Tien** boat landing. Board one of the frequent squarish red boats that go to **Wat Arun** (open daily 7am–5pm). In

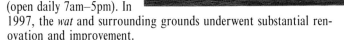

1997, the *wat* and surrounding grounds underwent substantial renovation and improvement.

During the Ayutthaya period, Wat Arun, or the Temple of Dawn, was a 15-m (50-ft) tall spire. It was restored by Rama II, III and IV, and the height of its central tower raised to its present 104m (341ft), making it one of the tallest religious structures in the country. At the bases of the four upper staircases are niches with statues depicting the four important events in the Buddha's life. Climb the eastern staircase for a grand view of the city. From here you also have a good view of the four *prang* (spires) that mark the corners of the courtyard. The tiny god on his white horse is Phra Pai, god of the wind. Look closely at one of the prangs: the flowers are fashioned from porcelain shards and seashells.

Recross the river by boat, walk to the main street, turn right at the next intersection, and turn left and walk to the entrance of **Wat Po** (open daily 8am–5pm). Wat Po predates the birth of Bangkok by a century. Restored many times, it is one of Bangkok's most eclectic *wat* and well worth a stroll.

Of special interest is the 45-m (107-ft) long, gilded **Reclining Buddha** in the northwest corner. Inspect its feet with the 108 signs, or *laksana,* by which a Buddha can be recognized, rendered in intricate mother-of-pearl patterns. In the courtyard are statues of various *rusi* (ascetics) demonstrating body exercises. (Wat Po is highly regarded as a centre of traditional medicine.)

Do not miss the *bot* to the right of the entrance with its marvellous mother-of-pearl doors and its sandstone bas-relief panels depicting scenes from the *Ramakien*. On the eastern side of the courtyard is the **School of Traditional Massage**. You pay a few hundred baht for an hour-long massage that will soothe travel-weary muscles. Thai masseurs dig in a little deeper but enduring their efforts will result in a truly relaxed body. You may be hungry by now; consider heading back to Tha Tien boat landing for noodles.

A Buddha image in a serene pose

3. Golden Mount and Surroundings

Sunrise on the Golden Mount; the Bird Market; the village where the monks' bowls (baht) are made; Loha Prasad; the Buddha amulet market; and a catfish lunch.

Another sunrise, this one with a panoramic view of the city. Tell the taxi driver to take you to the **Golden Mount** (Phu Khao Thong), for many years the highest point in the city. The stairs to the top begin at the southern base of this artificial hill. Climb through fragrant frangipani boughs, pausing for breath to look at the inscriptions on crypts containing ashes of deceased donors to **Wat Saket** (open daily 7.30am– 6pm), the tired temple at the hill's base. Built during the Ayutthaya period, Wat Saket was the city's charnel house during the cholera epidemics in the 19th century, with bodies laid out on its pavements for the vultures to eat.

The 318 steps up to the Golden Mount end at a room containing a Buddha image. The sign says it opens at 7.30am but it is usually open earlier. Enjoy the sunrise through the open windows or climb one more flight of stairs to the upper terrace dominated by the gilded *stupa* that gives the hill its name. Look north to see the city moat and part of the city wall: you will be going there later.

When sated, descend and exit through the gate. Turn right into a narrow lane that leads to Boriphat Road. Exit and turn left. At the next intersection, cross **Bamrung Muang Road** and turn left, walking about 50m to a small street with a sign designating it as Soi Ban Baht. Walk to the first intersection and then right, down an unpaved road into what appears to be a junkyard. Then begin listening for the sound of tapping hammers.

You are now in the village of **Ban Baht**, the only one of many craft villages that once existed within the city's confines. It is a poor area – some would call it a slum – but its residents share a common purpose: to pound 8 flat sheets of metal into a round *baht*, the bowl that monks carry on their morning alms rounds.

Retrace your steps. On reaching Boriphat Road, turn right and walk to the intersection. Turn left and cross the canal. Turn right to Maha Chai Road and walk 200m (656ft) to the city wall. At the second entryway, turn right. Along the way you will have passed two *wat* on the left. The first, Wat Thep Thidaram, is

Gilded stupa atop the Golden Mount

Wat Ratchanadda (foreground) and Loha Prasad

of minor interest. The second is Wat Ratchanadda, which you will visit a little later. The first thing that will strike you are dozens of beautiful bird cages containing singing doves, some of which are valued at more than 100,000 baht. The doves often compete at contests to see which can coo the prettiest song, with the winner's owner taking home huge cash prizes.

Exit the same doorway you entered. Cross the street towards a pyramidal pink building that sits behind Wat Ratchanadda. This is **Loha Prasad**, the Iron Monastery, so-called for the metal spires which rise from it. It was modelled after a monastery built in India about 1,500 BC. Noted for its odd architecture, the structure is usually closed to the public.

Now walk towards **Wat Ratchanadda** (open daily 6am–6pm) and see the interior walls of its *viharn*, covered with lovely murals depicting heaven and hell. If the doors are closed, ask a monk if you can peek inside.

In front of Wat Ratchanadda is an **amulet market**. Strictly speaking, the amulets on sale here have more to do with animism and magic than with the teachings of the Buddha. Nonetheless, the images, mostly that of the Buddha, are strung on gold necklaces and worn by many Thais. Some are said to protect the wearer from knife wounds, others from bullets. Many Thais are avid collectors, displaying the same fanatic attention to detail and arcane history as stamp collectors.

A string of amulet bracelets

36

Look for the small carved wooden penises which men wear on a string around their waists to ensure their virility.

Lunch is just up the street. Walk north to the Maha Chai intersection with Ratchadamnoen Avenue. Turn left and walk to the circle dominated by the Democracy Monument. On the right corner is **Pichitr Restaurant**. Try the *yam pladook foo*, catfish steamed, then deep fried and served with a tangy sauce.

4. By Boat up Khlong Bang Noi

Long-tailed boat trip up Khlong Bang Noi, passing through a cross-section of Thai life and back.

This trip – intended to whet your appetite for further adventures deep into the canals on the west side of the Chao Phraya river – can be taken in the afternoon but it is cooler in the morning and you will be doing some walking. Be sure to take along a pair of sunglasses and a hat. On this journey, you hurtle through the *khlongs* (canals) on a *rua hang yao* or 'long-tailed boat', so-called because of their long propeller shafts. These long, low and narrow boats, which are noisy and fast, serve as transportation up and down the *khlong* of Thonburi for the Thais. They are a bit cramped for *farang* (foreigners) with long legs – you may spend much of the journey with your chin on your knees – but what

Be careful of canal-spray

they lack in comfort they more than make up with scenery. Best of all, a return journey costs just 30 baht.

Take a taxi to the **Tha Tien landing** (the landing for the boat to Wat Arun). You want to go to the smaller landing to the right, where you will see several long-tailed boats moored. Ask to go to **Bang Noi** (not Bangkok Noi, which is another canal). Boats leave at 6.30 and 7.30am, and then hourly from 9am until 9pm. It is best to start at 7.30 or 9am at the latest.

The 30-minute cruise takes you past houses, boats laden with charcoal and vegetables on their way to the market, people living under bridges, birds, old *wat*, beautiful heliconia and canna lilies, orchid nurseries, and the people of Thonburi up and about in the morning. In other words, you slice through a cross-section of Thai life in the space of half an hour.

The trip ends in the middle of nowhere when the driver simply turns the boat around and heads back to Bangkok. Don't worry about repeating the journey; you'll be surprised how much you missed seeing on the way up.

5. National Museum

Guided tour of the treasures of the National Museum, followed by lunch at a riverside restaurant.

The **National Museum** (Wednesday to Sunday 9am–4pm) is one of the largest in Southeast Asia and displays a wide range of artefacts. The collection, which takes you on a journey into Thailand's fabled past, includes huge, gold-encrusted royal funeral chariots, weapons for elephant warfare, beautiful puppets, textiles and images of Buddha and Hindu gods, and other Thai exotica.

Guided 2-hour tours on subjects ranging from Buddhism to Thai art and culture are available in the mornings at 9.30am. The schedule of multi-language tours is as follows: Buddhism (English), every Wednesday; Thai art, religion and culture (English), every Thursday; Pre-Thai art (French), every Wednesday; Thai art and culture (German), every Thursday. (Tours are also available in Japanese.) Call 2241333 or 2241404 for details.

Besides housing a vast collection of antiquities, the museum has an interesting history of its own. The oldest buildings in the compound date from 1782 and were built as the palace of the so-called second king, a sort of deputy ruler and a feature of the Thai monarchy until 1870. Originally, the palace included a large park that went all the way to Wat Mahathat and covered the northern half of the present Sanam Luang grounds. Be sure to visit the **Buddhaisawan Chapel**, to the right of the ticket office of the museum, for its exquisite collection of murals, and for one of the three revered Phra Sihing Buddha statues in the country. The image is taken down and paraded through the streets of Bangkok each year on the day before the festival of Songkran, when water flies freely (see *Calendar of Special Events*).

After the tour, exit the museum to the left, and turn left again at the corner. Cross the bridge over the Chao Phraya River. Have lunch at the **Rim Nam Restaurant** on the Thonburi bank before you return to your hotel.

Discover Thailand's rich history at the National Museum

Chinese 'hell' money and assorted paraphernalia

6. Chinatown

A walk through Chinatown, a visit to a Chinese Buddhist temple, and a market straight out of ancient China.

This route takes you straight north through the heart of Chinatown. Take a boat or a taxi to the **Tha Ratchawong** landing on Ratchawong Road. If you have not had breakfast, stop at one of the sidewalk restaurants for a bowl of noodles. Then, walk about 50m to Songwat Road, which runs to the right. The corner is marked by a beautiful grey-and-green trading firm whose architecture is a blend of Moorish and German.

Turn right into Songwat Road, which parallels the waterfront. Songwat feels different from other city streets, exuding the air of old-time mercantile trading. At this hour of the morning, it is likely to be very quiet. Walk

Dried goods litter this Chinese shopfront

200m to the Chinese temple, **San Chao Kao** (Old Shrine), on the left and fronted by a car park. Just before it is Soi Isara Nuphap. Continue down this lane, all the way to its end.

Along the lane is an entrance to the *san chao* and just beyond it is a beautiful colonial-style old school. You then pass spice shops with sticks of cinnamon and other herbs; you will know from their heady fragrances. Near the end of the lane is a shop on the right making Chinese lanterns; watch the artists at work and then buy a pair for about 300 baht.

From here on, I'll give directions only; you make your own discoveries. Amidst the crowds and heat, you might feel lost, but worry not. Cross Soi Wanit 1. On your right, about 40m (43 yds) at 369/1 is another lovely shrine; step inside for a few minutes. Continue down the *soi* past the shops selling shrimp crackers and past the entrance to **Talad Kao** (Old Market). You can stop here if you wish, but as you'll be visiting another market, Talad Mai, later on, continue on to one of Chinatown's arteries: **Yaowarat Road**.

Cross this road and buy a fat Chinese apple or persimmon from one of the stalls. About 60m (65 yds) later, turn right into **Phutalet Market**, also known as **Talad Mai** (New Market). The market is a bit scruffy but is rich with the scents of seafood, Chinese foodstuffs and pastries, and has a medieval European feel to it. Buy a slice of pastry and sit down for a cup of coffee at one of the food-shops that ring the market and watch the activities.

Retrace your steps to Soi Isara Nuphap, turn right and continue north. Cross Charoen Krung (New Road). You are now in an area that more than any other section of the city, breathes of old China. Here, you will find paper funeral clothes, huge incense sticks, shrines, paper money, and dozens of other fascinating items which recall another age and land. The lane is filled with such shops. At its end, you come to **Phlab Phla Chai Road**. Here are shops selling doll-size houses and other items made of paper, a Chinese artform called *kong tek*. The Chinese burn these *kong tek* items, sending them to the afterlife to serve their deceased relatives.

Continue along Phlab Phla Chai. Just past **Wat Kanikaphon** on your left are two doors, recessed in the sidewalk stalls, bearing a pair of giant Chinese warriors who guard the **Mahayana Buddhist San Chao Dtai Hong Kong**. Enter it. (The main entrance is at the corner just ahead.) If you are lucky, you may be able to photograph people burning *kong tek* items in a tall furnace. If not, watch the

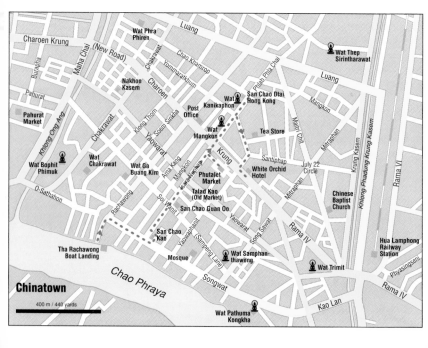

The scents of old China

devotees lighting candles and paying obeisance in a manner quite unlike that of the Thais. To get good candid shots of devotees praying, position yourself behind the shrine to the right side of the gate next to the furnace. A word of warning: the Chinese are shy about having their photos taken. Ask first.

Return to the mouth of Soi Isara Nuphap, but this time turn left, heading down Phlab Phla Chai back towards Charoen Krung.

Along this street are several stores selling Chinese tea in shiny canisters inscribed with large characters. Savour the scents of ancient China and buy whatever blend interests you. Have lunch at a sidewalk noodle stall or continue to Yaowarat and turn left. A few metres down is the **White Orchid Hotel**, which has a good air-conditioned Chinese restaurant on its mezzanine.

7. Prasart Museum

A fascinating stroll through an art collector's private palace.

An art collector's dream to house his prized artefacts in a classical setting has resulted in the **Prasart Museum** (Friday to Sunday 10am–3pm), a small complex of superb buildings in a countryside garden. Many of the buildings are themselves works of art, transported from distant villages.

The collection runs from pre-historic pieces to those of the present dynasty, with special emphasis on *bencharong* (five-colour) pottery. Gilded Chinese screens and beds, mother-of-pearl receptacles and Buddha images complete the collection. In recreating the settings for the items, the owner employed craftsmen to restore old shutters and paint numerous new ones in painstaking detail. The garden is filled with old Chinese stone carvings.

The museum is located in a distant eastern corner of Bangkok's suburbs; taxi drivers are usually reluctant to go there. The museum's address is 9 Soi Krungthep Kreetha 4A, Krungthep Kreetha Road, Bangkapi, beyond Hua Mark (tel: 3793601/3793607). The entrance fee includes a guide, and tea or coffee.

8. Chatuchak Weekend Market

Browse in one of Asia's great bazaars with everything imaginable.

The Oriental bazaar is something of a legend, and few markets in Asia meet the definition as well as the **Chatuchak weekend market**, on the northern end of the city. Within the market's narrow lanes are found all the colours, scents and sounds of Asia.

Chatuchak's gates open at 6am and close at 6pm – and only on weekends, of course. Because it can be unbearably hot by midday, try and get there early. Take a taxi or air-conditioned bus No 2, 3, 9, 10, or 13 and ask to get off at Chatuchak. The bus will stop just beyond a pedestrian overpass. Walk back to the gate and head for the interesting clock tower in the middle of the market. (Don't be confused by the simpler-looking clock tower in a nearby park.) This short walk alone will give you the flavour of the market; maps at all of the entrances indicate in both Thai and English where different commodities are sold.

Guiding you through Chatuchak is like trying to lead through a maelstrom. It is better to let your senses take you where they will. I will give general directions and then you are on your own. Walk behind the clock tower to the second turning on the right. You will hear puppies yapping and cocks' crowing in what for most people is the most interesting section of the market: the animal stalls. Puppies, rabbits, flying squirrels, brightly-coloured parrots and cockatoos and other winged, webbed and footed creatures inhabit this giant pet store. There are tanks of goby, goldfish and carp. Look for the rows of iridescent blue and red Siamese Fighting Fish inside glass jars and separated by a piece of cardboard.

Continue towards the back of the market and turn left – south – to enter the pottery section and the start of the stalls selling fake antiques. Farther on are Thai handicrafts and more art objects, as well as coins and stamps. East of this section is a huge selection of casual clothes at bargain prices.

At lunchtime, head for the terminus and the No 12 air-conditioned bus. Behind it is the famous **Vegetarian Restaurant**. Operated by Bangkok's former mayor, the restaurant is open from 6am to 2pm, Tuesday to Sunday. The delicious vegetarian dishes sell for around 15 baht per plate, together with a glass of cold soybean milk.

Cute figurines like these are aplenty at Chatuchak

9. Through Chinatown's Heart

A leisurely lunch on the terrace at River City, then window shopping for antiques and a walk down historic Sampeng Lane to Wat Chakrawat's crocodile pond.

Gain a different perspective on Chinatown by walking along the lane where it all began 200 years ago. Start with a seafood lunch at the **Savoey Seafood Restaurant**, on the terrace of the **River City** shopping complex next to the Royal Orchid Sheraton Hotel. Savoey's speciality is seafood cooked Chinese-style, in keeping with the Chinese theme of this itinerary. Choose from a variety of seafood displayed on the bed of chipped ice and it will be prepared to your taste. Especially good is their roasted crab meat with noodles. After lunch, wander through River City's dozens of antique shops. Even if you aren't an antique aficionado, you'll be tempted.

About 3pm, exit River City and walk left along **Soi Wanit 2**, a small alley just past the multi-level car park. After 50m (55 yds), turn left into the riverside church, **Wat Kalawa** (Rosary Church). If you had difficulties finding it, just ask the people in the neighbourhood. Peek inside to get a glimpse of its soaring wooden ceiling and see how Thai Catholics have modified a traditional cathedral.

Continue down Soi Wanit 1, which turns into a car-parts recycling neighbourhood, keeping to the left at a confusing intersection. At the T-intersection further on, with heaps of old engines on the left and an immense shade tree opposite, turn right into **Soi Phanu Rang Si**; 50m (55 yds) on, turn left and walk another 50m (55 yds). The temple on your left is the 300-year-old **Wat Pathuma Kongkha**. The *wat* sits on what was once the execution site for royal criminals. The *wat* has some Chinese statuary and stucco decorations.

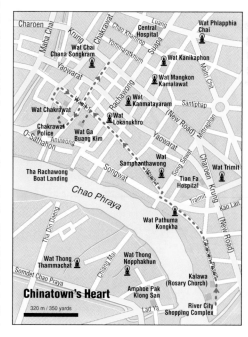

Exit the *wat*, turn left and continue on. About 100m (109 yds) beyond the *wat*, angle right and into Soi Wanit 1. This is the famous **Sampeng Lane**, now renamed and vastly tamed. (One might also forgo the previous sections, and join here from the Tha Song Sawat river landing.) At the turn of the century, this area was a maze of alleys inhabited mainly by Chinese merchants. It contained opium dens, gambling parlours and the so-called 'green light' houses, the green lanterns being the equivalent of red lights in similar districts elsewhere. Most of the goods along the *soi* are sold wholesale, but there is a wide variety of retail items as well. The lane starts out quietly, but quickly narrows into a packed walkway.

At the intersection of **Soi Mangkon** (also called Sanjao Mai) is the handsome facade of the old Gold Exchange. At the next intersection, cross busy Ratchawong Road and continue 50m (55 yds) to a small alley on the left amidst textile shops and marked by a red modern sign that says 'Shay Inter'. Enter the alley and at the T-junction, turn right and walk straight into the courtyard of one of Chinatown's oldest *wat*, **Ga Buang Kim**. Note the scenes on the wall by the main door.

The grotto at Wat Chakrawat

Return to Soi Wanit 1 and walk to the next major thoroughfare, Chakrawat. Turn left and walk some 80m (87 yds) to the entrance of **Wat Chakrawat**. This hodgepodge of buildings has several attractions. Walk about 70m (77 yds) to the ornate gate on your left. Enter and turn right to an interesting grotto enclosing the 1-m (3-ft) high statue of a fat man. According to local legend, the statue was built to honour a devout but very handsome monk who was frequently pestered by women while deep in meditation. His response was to stuff himself until he became so fat that women eventually lost interest – and desire – for him.

Exit the grotto and return almost to the gate before crossing the makeshift carpark to an enclosed pond, which sits between the two *prang*. In it are several crocodiles, said to be progeny of 'One-Eyed Guy', a half-blind croc which once terrorised the canals but retired here years ago.

Temples, incidentally, also serve as animal asylums. When people have a litter of puppies they don't want, they often take them to the *wat*, where the animals will be fed on leftovers from the monks' meals. It is a little odd to drop off a crocodile, but that is what someone once did here. Other temples get elephants and cats.

Exit the gate and turn left, continuing to a gate that leads from the *wat* into **Soi Khlong Thom**. Turn left. Cross Soi Wanit 1 and continue on to the intersections with Yaowarat Road and farther on with Charoen Krung (New Road), where you can catch a taxi or a bus home.

Face of old China

10. Suan Pakkad and Jim Thompson House

Visit two palatial teakwood houses built in classical Thai style.

Before the Thais eschewed wood for concrete, they evolved an architectural style all their own, one which blended into the tropical surroundings and took full advantage of the breezes. The following are two quite different examples of old-fashioned Thai homes.

Whimsically named **Suan Pakkad**, or the Cabbage Patch (352 Sri Ayutthaya Road; open Monday to Saturday 9am–4pm), this was the residence of the Prince of Nagor Svarga and his wife Princess Chumbhot. The teak houses were transported from the north and erected around a pond stalked by pelicans. Wander through the complex, pausing to look at the fine Ayutthaya-period manuscript cabinets, with their lacquer decorations and other items in the art collection. The princess was an avid collector of Ban Chiang pottery and neolithic artefacts, housed in the back building on the right.

Suan Pakkad's centrepiece is the **Lacquer Pavilion**, one of the finest examples of priceless gold-and-black lacquer work in Asia. It has been reconstructed from two *ho trai* or monastic libraries. The interior walls are richly decorated with Buddhist scenes. Note the depiction of 17th-century European visitors wearing plumed hats and riding fat horses. Adjacent to Suan Pakkad is the **Chumbhot–Pantip Centre of Arts**, with changing exhibits.

Like Suan Pakkad, the **Jim Thompson House** (Soi Kasem San 2 on Rama I Road across from the National Stadium; open Monday to Saturday 9am–5pm) is an assemblage of six Ayutthayan teak houses to create the archetypal Thai-style house. Built just after World War II, the house is stunning with its peaceful garden setting and art collection. An American intelligence officer in World War II, Thompson made his fortune by introducing exotic Thai silk to the Western world. Thompson's life was as mysterious as was his disappearance in the late 1960s in the Malaysian jungles of Cameron Highlands while on a Sunday afternoon walk.

There are also superb reproductions of old maps and wall hangings for sale on the ground floor. The admission ticket includes a guided tour in English or French.

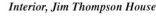

Interior, Jim Thompson House

Heading upriver to Nonthaburi

11. Nonthaburi

A ride upriver; lunch at a floating restaurant; a provincial market; the beautiful riverside Wat Chalerm Phra Kiet; and a bus or boat ride home through the back country.

This afternoon takes you out of the city to experience river scenery and a rural temple. Plan to leave between 11am and noon so you can have lunch in Nonthaburi. It begins with a long ride up the Chao Phraya River. Catch an express boat (the long, low white ones with red trim) at any of the landings along the river. Make sure the boat is travelling to your right. The boat ride takes about one hour to the upriver terminus at **Nonthaburi**. Along the way you will see houses on stilts, sawmills, and picturesque riverside temples.

Disembark at Nonthaburi – no sign in English but there is a proper landing with a clock tower – and turn right along the promenade past the wooden provincial offices and the lamp posts bearing *durian* when they are in season. Nonthaburi is famous for this thorny ambrosial fruit; whether you love or hate this fruit, it's impossible to be impartial.

A durian vendor

At the end of the seawall is a **floating restaurant** where you can dine on Thai seafood. It's the only restaurant at the end of the promenade.

Return to the dock, explore the market and then catch a ferry to the other side of river. Hop onto a motorcycle taxi or a *tuk tuk* and ask the driver to take you to the **Wat Chalerm Phra Kiet**. A few minutes later, you arrive at what seems to be a fortress wall in the middle of nowhere. After making sure that the driver waits for you, enter the back door to reach a garden that is filled with Chinese statues. Made of wood and tree roots, these statues have been fashioned into the shapes of Chinese gods, including that most un-Chinese of all deities: Santa Claus. From the garden, enter the *wat*, one of the most beautiful to be found anywhere in Bangkok, as much for its architecture as for its remote setting. The tall *chedi* stands behind a *bot* (ordination hall) that is flanked by two *viharn* or sermon halls, all of which have been restored. The gables are covered in ceramic tiles dating back to the reign of King Rama III (1824–1851), when Chinese design was in vogue.

After admiring the fine paintings (if the doors are closed, ask a monk to open them), walk through the riverside gateway and into a compound of raintrees. Walk through the compound to the twin wooden *sala*, or pavilions, on either side of a concrete *sala* where you can enjoy a view of the river.

Return to the ferry boat pier. Three bus lines run from here into the countryside; you want the bus to Bang Kruai. The

20-minute trip through lovely rural areas terminates in the town of **Bang Kruai**. The bus stops opposite Wat Chalaw. Get off, cross the street and walk through the gate of **Wat Chalaw** to see work in progress on one of the most ambitious architectural undertakings to be found in Thailand.

On the left, a *bot* is being built in the shape of the massive *Sri Suphannahongse*, the principal Royal Barge (see *Itinerary 12*). At 95m (103yds) long, the *bot* is twice the length of the original vessel. It will take years to complete and the mirror mosaics already in place suggest that the *bot* is going to be a spectacular structure.

To return to the city, walk to the canal on the far side of the *wat* compound. You can either hire a flat-bottomed speedboat (the fare must be bargained; usually about 100 baht, regardless of the number of passengers) which will zip you down the canal on a hair-raising trip, or catch the regular long-tailed boat that travels down Khlong Bangkok Noi to the Tha Chang boat landing next to the Grand Palace.

12. Canal Cruise and the Royal Barge Museum

A journey into the canals for a flavour of riverside life and a visit to the Royal Barge Museum.

Plan to arrive at the Oriental Hotel at about 2pm. Walk past the entrance and down the driveway to a lane on the left that runs between the hotel and a wall to a small boat landing. You want to rent a motor launch (*rua mai*) – not a long-tailed boat. The launch, with its low roof, chugs along at a sedate pace and seats 8 to 10 people comfortably. The price will depend on your bargaining ability, but it should not cost you more than 300 baht an hour.

The boat will travel upriver past Wat Arun and the Grand Palace

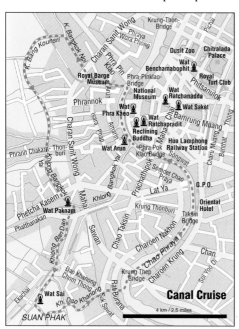

Canal Cruise

before entering **Khlong Bangkok Noi**. A little after turning into the wide *khlong*, and just before reaching a bridge, ask the driver to stop at the **Royal Barge Museum** (open daily 8.30am–4.30pm), located on your right. Displayed here are the most important vessels in the 51-barge royal fleet, which undertakes grand river processions on special occasions, the last in 1996, the 50th anniversary of the king's monarchy. The oldest and most beautiful barge with the graceful, bird-like head and long beak is called the *Sri Suphannahongse*. Built during the reign of Rama I (1782–1809) and repaired during that of Rama VI (1910–1925), the boat was built from a single piece of teak 44m (45yd) long. Continue up the canal until **Khlong Chak Phra**, then left. Among the palm trees are many beautiful old houses. Khlong Chak Phra changes its name to **Khlong Bang Kounsri** and then to **Khlong Bangkok Yai**. If sated, continue along Bangkok Yai, re-enter the Chao Phraya River and finish at the Oriental Hotel.

To extend your cruise, turn right from Bangkok Yai into **Khlong Ban Dan**. Next is **Wat Sai**, followed by the jungled area of Suan Phak. Turn left into **Khlong Bang Mod**, then **Khlong Dao Khanong**, re-entering the river below **Krung Thep Bridge**. Head upriver and end at the Oriental Hotel.

Be on your guard when bargaining

48

13. Thai Boxing

An afternoon of Thai boxing and a Northeastern-cuisine dinner.

Thai boxing is not everyone's favourite sport, but it is worth attending as much for the graceful movements as for the mayhem among the high rollers in the audience. Of the two stadiums in Bangkok, **Lumpini Stadium** (at Rama IV Road) and **Ratchadamnoen Stadium** at Ratchadamnoen Nok Avenue (next to the Tourism Authority of Thailand office), the latter is the older. The Sunday matinee at 4pm is recommended, as it offers the cheapest seats, but there are also bouts on Monday and Wednesday at 6pm, and Thursday at 5pm and 9pm.

No-holds-barred Thai boxing

Ten bouts are presented, each comprising five three-minute rounds. With fighters using their elbows, knees, feet and fists and sometimes all at once, it's not surprising that most matches end before all 10 bouts are completed. The mystical dance each boxer performs before his fight pays homage to his teacher; the orchestra which plays loud raucous music serves to spur on the combatants.

Afterwards, exit to the right onto the road that goes behind the stadium to the strip of Northeastern food restaurants. The third one on the right, **Pon Charoen** at 76/5, is my favourite. Order barbecued chicken (*gai yang*), minced pork (*larb nua*), beef jerky (*nua yang*) and glutinous rice (*khao niew*), and wash it all down with icy-cold Singha beer.

14. Lak Muang and Surroundings

Pavement astrologers; the city pillar and free drama performances; Wat Ratchapradit; Wat Ratchabophit; Wat Suthat; Giant Swing for sunset photos.

This tour takes you to some lesser-known *wat* in the vicinity of Wat Phra Kaeo. Start from the **Royal Hotel** at about 1pm. Cross the canal and angle left down Ratchadamnoen Avenue towards Wat Phra Kaeo (the Emerald Buddha). Just past the canal is the **statue of Mae Thorani**, the goddess who wrung water from her hair and washed away the army of demons who were harassing the Buddha while he was meditating to reach enlightenment.

Farther on are astrologers who work from their makeshift offices on the pavement. Most don't speak English, so it is

Pavement astrologer

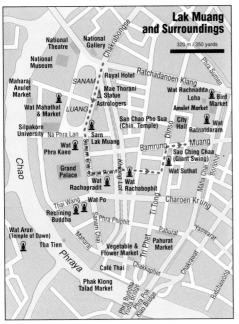

Lak Muang and Surroundings

320 m / 350 yards

little use asking for a prediction, but observe the many ways, ranging from palmistry to numerology, by which they tell and sell fortunes. The astrologers also employ birds to pick a card from among a pack of fortune-telling cards (see if you can spot the sleight of hand).

At the corner, the ornate single-storey building on your left is **Lak Muang**, residence of the city's guardian spirit. Built in the late 1700s and the first structure erected by King Rama I, the building contains two rather phallic-looking columns. These *lingam* structures are associated with the Hindu god Siva, many images of whom occupy the shrine. The Lak Muang is regarded as the foundation stone of the capital, the place where the city's guardian deity lives and the point from which the power of the city emanates. Distances in Bangkok are measured from this stone. Thais frequently pray to the Lak Muang for divine aid, beseeching the spirits for success in jobs, the lottery or marriage. If you wish, buy a candle and incense and do the same. Then, walk outside to watch the dance performances.

Exit Lak Muang and head towards the handsome **Defence Ministry** with its antique cannons. At the second street, Saranrom Road, turn left. Halfway down on the right is **Wat Ratchapradit** (open daily 8am–5pm). This little *wat* is an interesting study in the architectural styles of Asia. The *bot* (ordination hall), clad in grey Chinese marble, is attended by a Khmer-style *prang* (an Ayutthayan-style *chedi* or *stupa*) on the left and a Bayon-style *prang*, which dates from 12th-century Angkor Thom in Cambodia, on the right. Behind the *bot* is a *stupa* in the Singhalese style of Sri Lanka. Ask a monk to open the *bot* doors so you can stand back and admire the 19th-century murals depicting the royal ceremonies for each of the 12 months of the year.

Head back on to Saranrom Road, turn right and walk to the canal with a golden statue of a pig on the bank. This tribute represents the birth year in the Buddhist 12-year cycle of King Chulalongkorn's consort,

Buddha image outside Wat Ratchapradit

Wat Suthat is home to Thailand's tallest viharn (sermon hall)

Queen Saowapha. Cross the footbridge and continue on until the street name changes to Ratchabophit Road. On the corner is a cemetery, with Gothic monuments, holding ashes of noble families. Halfway along on the right is **Wat Ratchabophit** (open daily 8am–8pm), another jewel-box temple of intriguing design. Built in 1870 by Rama V (1868–1910), the temple's tall *chedi* is enclosed in a circular cloister clad in *bencharong* ceramic tiles and incorporating the *bot*. Note the doors of the *bot*: mother-of-pearl depictions of insignias of the five royal ranks. The *bot* interior is a miniature Gothic cathedral, reflecting the Thai fascination with foreign styles.

On exiting the *wat*, turn right. Continue past the intersection with Fuang Nakhorn and on to the T-junction with Ti Thong Road. Turn left and walk to the next intersection, turn right and, halfway down, turn right again into **Wat Suthat**, (open daily 8am–6pm) Bangkok's tallest *viharn* (sermon hall). Its beautiful front and back doors were carved by King Rama II.

Inside is an 8-m (26-ft) tall Buddha image brought from Sukhothai and surrealistic mural paintings depicting the last 24 *Chadoks* or incarnations of the man who was eventually born as the Buddha. The courtyard contains extraordinary Chinese bronze horses, stone statues and pagodas carried as ballast in rice ships travelling from China.

Exit Wat Suthat and look at the **Giant Swing**. The huge teak posts, and the swing (which is no longer there) were erected for a Brahmin ceremony to honour the god Siva. Until it was banned in the 1940s, the annual ceremony involved pairs of men propelling a swing to great heights to snatch a bag of gold from a tall pole.

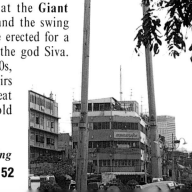

The now-empty frame of the Giant Swing

15. Snake Farm and Lumpini Park

Buffet lunch at Tiara Room overlooking the city; Snake Farm; an astrologer; coffee with a view; Lumpini in the evening.

Start with a feast and a spectacular view of the city from the Tiara Room atop the **Dusit Thani Hotel**. You may want to linger over this sumptuous buffet, so start about noon; the next event on the

schedule gets underway at 2pm. It will be a lazy afternoon, so eat to your heart's content. From the Tiara, you look down on Lumpini Park, the traffic (the best way to experience it), Silom Road and the Rama IX Bridge to the south.

After lunch, walk left down Rama IV Road. Pass the Surawong Road intersection and cross at the Montien Hotel to the government-run **Queen Saowapha Institute**, formerly called the Pasteur Institute and better known as the **Snake**

A cobra ready to strike

Farm (Monday to Friday 8.30am–4.40pm, Saturday and Sunday 8.30am–noon; snake feeding and venom-extracting demonstrations at 10.30am and 2pm Monday to Friday, and 10.30am on weekends and holidays). The institute, the second-oldest in the world, produces anti-venom serum from seven types of poisonous snakes: king cobra, Siamese cobra, banded kraits, Russell's viper, Malayan pit viper and the green and Pope's pit vipers. The Snake Farm is part of the Thai Red Cross, and where one can have hepatitis, smallpox and typhoid inoculations as well as rabies treatment, not to mention anonymous tests for sexually-transmitted diseases.

When finished, recross the street to the **Montien Hotel**. On the mezzanine floor are professional astrologers who for 400 baht will

tell your fortune using numerology or palmistry. If you visit near the 15th or 30th of the month, ask for a lucky lottery number. Then buy a ticket from a street vendor. When satisfied that your future is rosy, walk back up Rama IV to Robinson's Department Store on the corner of Silom. As the sun sets, cross to the opposite corner to **Lumpini Park**. If the park wears a Chinese face in the morning, in the afternoon it is a Thai domain. Boys

Afternoon delight at Lumpini

play soccer and *takraw* (a rattan ball game); entire families sit on mats to enjoy the shade and snacks sold by vendors. Row a boat or fly a kite. When it becomes dark, head for your hotel, if so inclined.

Excursions

16. Ancient City

A half-day trip to the Ancient City, a microcosm of Thailand's great temples and palaces.

The **Ancient City** (open daily 8am–5pm) is a philanthropist's gift to Thailand, a 80-ha (200-acre) park containing one-third-sized replicas of the kingdom's principal temples and palaces. An enormous undertaking spanning the past 20 years, each monument in the park has been carefully replicated in precise detail. Even the shape of the park corresponds to the map of Thailand, with the attractions appropriately sited. To get there, take air-conditioned bus No. 8 or 11 to the clocktower in the town of **Paknam**, south of Bangkok. Then catch minibus No. 38 to the gate of the complex. Alternatively, several tour companies operate half-day coach tours for a fee.

17. Ayutthaya

A full-day guided tour of Bang Pa-in and the ancient capital of Ayutthaya. Includes a cruise and lunch or dinner.

The former capital of **Ayutthaya**, 60km (40 miles) upriver from Bangkok, is filled with beautiful old architecture. Its magnificent temples and palaces, and more than 2,000 gleaming golden spires, impressed early European visitors who filled their journals with paeans to its glory. Destroyed in 1767 by the Burmese, even in ruins Ayutthaya evokes the majesty of one of Asia's great empires. The best way to approach it is as the first European explorers did in the 1660s: by boat up the Chao Phraya River, preferably aboard a luxury cruiser like the *Oriental Queen*.

The *Oriental Queen* leaves the Oriental Hotel at 8am, cruising past the city's major landmarks. It stops at **Bang Sai Handicrafts Centre**, created by Queen Sirikit to preserve ancient arts, and then to **Bang Pa-in** to see the former Summer Palace and its mix of architectural styles. A buffet lunch on board is followed by a guided tour of Ayutthaya. Return by coach to Bangkok. Alternatively, you can take the coach to Ayutthaya and return by boat with dinner on board, a better choice because of the evening view of Bangkok from the river. You can make your bookings at the Oriental Hotel at tel: 2330400 or 2360420 ext 3133.

Reclining Buddha at Ayutthaya

18. Bridge on the River Kwai

By rail to the historic River Kwai; the Nakhon Pathom chedi and Kanchanaburi war cemetery. Full day.

State Railways of Thailand offers an economical day-trip to the **Death Railway** and the **River Kwai Bridge**. Departing **Hualampong Station** on Rama 4 Road at 6.35am, the train makes a stop at the world's tallest *chedi* at Nakhon Pathom and then at the bridge itself, so you can walk across it. The journey continues along the rickety railway through jungle and arrives at 11.30am at the terminus, **Nam Tok**, where you eat a delicious Thai lunch.

You have 2½ hours at Nam Tok to swim in the waterfall-fed pond or walk in the jungle. From Nam Tok station, return to **Kanchanaburi** to visit the war cemetery holding Allied POWs who died building the infamous bridge. Arrive at Hualampong Station by late evening. The ticket price includes lunch and refreshments. Book at Hualampong Station.

The other alternative is for you to book a combination air-conditioned bus and train journey with a local travel agent.

The infamous bridge

Shopping

In making shopping recommendations, I am guided less by my tastes than by my friends' preferences. Shopping in Bangkok can be a fascinating experience, but before you set yourself loose like children in a toy store, remember that most people end up buying more than they had planned, and are subsequently saddled with the problem of carting everything home.

Antiques and Reproductions

Wood, bronze, terracotta and stone images from all over Thailand and Burma abound in Bangkok's antique shops. You will also find carved wooden angels, mythical animals, temple bargeboards and eave brackets. Although the Thai government has banned the export of Buddha images, there are numerous statues of other deities and disciples which can be sent abroad. Bronze deer, angels and characters from the *Ramakien* cast in bronze do not fall under the export ban.

Hand-hewn wooden figurines

Chiang Mai produces beautiful wooden fakes modelled on antique sculptures. They make lovely home decor items and are sold as reproductions, with no attempt to pass them off as genuine antiques. Animals, Buddha's disciples and myriad other pieces range in size from miniatures to life-size.

Wooden furniture include cabinets, tables, dining room and bedroom sets, or something as simple as a wooden tray or trivet. The carving tends to be heavy and the pieces are generally large.

Baskets

Thailand's abundant vines and grasses are transformed into lamps, storage boxes, tables, colourful mats, handbags, letter holders, tissue boxes and slippers. Wicker and bamboo are turned into storage lockers with brass fittings and furniture to fill the entire house. Shops can provide the cushions as well.

Yan lipao, a sturdy grass about the thickness of a broomstraw, is woven into delicate patterns to create purses and bags for formal occasions. Although expensive, the bags are durable, retaining their beauty for years.

Ceramics

Best known among the array of distinctive Thai ceramics is celadon, usually fashioned into jade-green statues, lamps, ashtrays and other items distinguished by their glazed surfaces. Celadon is also tinted in dark green, brown and cobalt-blue hues.

Modelled after its Chinese cousin, blue-and-white porcelain includes pots, lamp bases, vases, household items and figurines. The quality varies widely depending on the skill of the artist, the firing and glazing techniques.

Bencharong (five colours) describes a style of porcelain that was derived from Chinese art in the 16th century. Normally reserved for bowls, containers and fine chinaware, its classic pattern is a small religious figure surrounded by intricate floral designs rendered in five colours – usually green, blue, yellow, rose and black.

Earthenware includes a wide assortment of pots, planters and dinner sets in a rainbow of colours and designs. Also popular are the brown-glazed Shanghai jars bearing yellow dragons, which the Thais fill with bath water. Visitors often buy these home as planters.

Decorative Arts

Presentation trays and containers as well as plaques bearing classical scenes are rendered in mother-of-pearl. Beware of craftsmen who take shortcuts by using black paint rather than the traditional seven layers of lacquer. On these items, the surface cracks, often while the item is still on the shelf.

Lacquerware comes in two varieties: the gleaming gold-and-black type, normally seen on the shutters of temple windows, and the

A potpourri of Thai ornaments and coins

matte red type with black and/or green details, which originated in northern Thailand and Burma. The selection of lacquerware includes ornate containers and trays, wooden figurines, woven bamboo baskets and Burmese-inspired Buddhist manuscript pages. The pieces may also be bejewelled with tiny glass mosaics and gilded ornaments.

Modern Thai artists produce everything from realistic to abstract paintings, the latter often a weak imitation of Western art. Two areas at which Thai artists excel are depictions of everyday life — although dismissed as tourist art, this genre contains some superb works — and of new interpretations of classical Buddhist themes.

Fabrics and Clothes

More than any other craft, Thai silk is synonymous with Thailand.

A big-headed mannequin

Brought to world attention by American entrepreneur Jim Thompson, Thai silk has enjoyed enduring popularity. It is sold in a wide variety of colours, its hallmark being the tiny nubs which, like embossings, rise from its surface.

Thai silk is an extremely versatile fabric. It is cut into suits by local tailors, but is more popular as blouses, ties and scarves. It is also used to cover everything from purses to picture frames. Lengths of Thai silk printed with elephant, bamboo, floral and dozens of other motifs are often turned into decorative cushion covers or used as upholstery.

Mudmee is a type of Northeastern silk whose hues are muted and its colours sombre. It is a form of tie-dyed cloth and is sold in lengths or as finished clothes. The fabric makes a very elegant woman's dress or suit, or the handsome, Nehru-necked *rajaprathan* favoured by Thai officials.

Thai cotton in plain colours and prints is made into dresses and most of the items into which Thai silk is rendered. Other cotton items are tablecloths, placemats and napkins. A surprising number of visitors arrive with measurements for sofas and windows and have shops tailor and ship upholstery and curtains.

Cotton is popular for shirts and dresses, since it is light and 'breathes' in Bangkok's hot, humid air. Although cotton is available in various lengths, it is generally sold as ready-made garments.

Gems and Jewellery

Thailand is a leading producer of rubies and sapphires. Connoisseurs (or those who know what they're doing) will find both rough cut and polished stones for a fraction of their cost overseas. Thailand is also regarded as the world's leader in cutting coloured gemstones and diamonds. Thai artisans set the stones in gold and silver to create jewellery and bejewelled containers of superb quality.

Light-green Burmese jade is especially popular and carved into jewellery and art objects. High quality cultured pearls set in gold are usually bought from the pearl farms of Phuket. If cash is in short supply, opt for costume jewellery, which is a major Thai craft with numerous items available. A related craft which has grown rapidly in the past decade is that of gilding fresh orchids in 22 karat gold.

A word of caution: Shop only at reputable stores. There are numerous and frequent instances of tourists being sold fake or overpriced goods, with promises of higher resale at their branches overseas.

Hill Tribe Crafts

The tribes of the northern hills produce a wide selection of brightly-coloured needlepoint work in geometric and floral patterns, which are used to decorate shirts, coats, bags and other personal items.

Hill-tribe silver work is valued less for its silver content (which is low) than for the intricate work and imagination that goes into making it. The variety includes necklaces, head-dresses, bracelets and rings worn on ceremonial occasions. Enhancing their value are the old British-Indian rupee coins which decorate the women's elaborate headdresses. Other hill tribe items include knives, baskets, pipes and gourd flutes that sound like bagpipes.

Home Decor Items

Thailand's handcrafted artificial flowers and fruits made of organza, poplin rayons, cotton, velvet, satin acetate, plastic, polyester and paper are virtually indistinguishable from the fresh garden variety.

Containers, vases, screens and tables are crafted in papier mâché as gift or home decor items. Burmese in manufacture and style, *kalaga* wall hangings depicting gods and mythical animals have gained immense popularity in the past few years. The figures are stuffed with cotton to make them stand out from the surface in bas-relief. Buy the hangings loose and have them framed at home.

Seashells, from Phuket and other southern islands, are used to decorate an assortment of lamp shades, boxes and picture frames. Also popular are the triangular pillows covered in red, blue and yellow striped cloth and accented by embroidery. These are used by Thais as backrests while sitting on the floor or even on a sofa.

Artificial silk blooms as good as the real stuff

Metal Art Objects

Although Thai craftsmen have produced some of Asia's most beautiful Buddha images, modern bronze sculpture tends to be of less exalted subjects. Minor deities, characters from the classical literary saga, the *Ramakien*, deer and abstract figures are cast up to 2m (5.6 ft) tall and are clad with annealed brass skins to make them gleam. Bronze is also cast into handsome cutlery. Small bronze temple bells can be hung in the house eaves to tinkle in the wind. More expensive are Laotian frog drums which are covered with glass plates and used as tables. Silver and gold are pounded into jewellery items, boxes and other decorative pieces and are often set with gems.

To create nielloware boxes and receptacles, a design is incised in silver and sometimes gold. The background is cut away and filled with an amalgam of dark metal, leaving the figures to stand up in high relief against the black or dark grey background.

Ornate Thai silverware

Tin, mined near Phuket, is the prime ingredient in pewterware, of which Thailand is a major producer. Items range from clocks and steins to egg cups and figurines.

Theatre Art Objects

Papier mâché *khon* masks, the kind used in palace dance and drama, are painted and lacquer decorations affixed and gilded. The quality of the shapes and the paintwork of such masks is evident at a quick glance.

Shadow puppets cut from the hides of water buffaloes and displayed on backlit screens in open-air theatres tell the *Ramakien* story. Check to be sure the figure is actually cut from hide and not from a sheet of black plastic. Also inspired by the *Ramakien*, craftsmen have fashioned miniature chariots and warriors in gilded wood or glass sculptures. The same technique is also employed to create reproductions of the famous Royal Barges.

Where to Buy

Although Bangkok produces only a fraction of Thailand's arts and crafts, it is the country's main marketplace for handicraft items. There are huge air-conditioned malls like **Amarin Plaza, Siam Centre, Mahboonkrong, Oriental Plaza**, **World Trade Centre, Seacon, Future Park, The Mall,** PATA and **Central Plaza,** filled with shops selling a wide variety of items. Some shopping centres are devoted to a single category of art, like the **River City** complex, which houses dozens of so-called antique shops, many with excellent replicas but some with real antiques.

Queen Sirikit's **Chitralada stores** sell the rare crafts she and her organisation, SUPPORT, have worked so diligently to preserve. There

Religious items on sale at Bamrung Muang Road

are branches in the airport, Grand Palace, Oriental Plaza, Hilton Hotel and Pattaya. The Thai government's handicraft centre, **Narayana Phand**, at 127 Ratchadamri Road, displays the full array of Thai handicrafts. Most major department stores have special handicraft departments with locally-crafted items. Charoen Krung, Silom, Surawong and Sukhumvit are lined with crafts shops. Sampeng Lane, the Thieves Market, the Buddha amulet markets at Tha Prajan, Wat Ratchanadda and the huge weekend market at **Chatuchak** are magnets that draw shoppers. Merchandising started in the streets and after going indoors now seems to be moving back to the streets again. At the lower end of Sukhumvit Road, in the lanes of Siam Square, Silom Road, Gaysorn Road and Ratchadamri Avenue, there are great bargains. Where else can you pick up a shirt for 150 baht?

Eating Out

Anyone who has tried Thai cuisine knows that it is not an idle boast to say that the food is one of the best in the world. The astonishing variety of flavours and textures ensures a wealth of dining experiences and provides an excellent excuse for a visit to Thailand. You could spend an entire holiday eating: a gourmet tour packed with a non-stop array of mouth-watering meals, although your tailor would never forgive you. And if for some peculiar reason you don't enjoy Thai food, there are cuisines from half the world to be found in Bangkok.

A Taste of Thailand

Thai dishes are as individual and varied as the cooks who prepare them. The curries are made with coconut milk, and although most are spicy, they can be made bland on request. Among the fiery favourites are *thom yam gung* (piquant soup with shrimp), *gaeng khiew wan gai* (a hot green curry with chicken or beef) and *gaeng phet* (a red curry with beef). Among the non-spicy dishes are: *thom kha gai* (coconut milk curry with chicken), *plaamuk thawd krathiem prik thai* (squid, or sometimes fish, fried with garlic and black pepper), *nua phat namman hoi* (beef in oyster sauce), *muu phat priew wan* (sweet and sour pork) and *homok talay* (a mildly spicy fish or seafood mousse). The Thais also make luscious sweets from coconut milk, tapioca and fruits, and a coconut-based frozen dessert called *ice cream kathit*. Some of the best Thai desserts are sold by pavement vendors. If you don't have a penchant for sweets, opt for a plate of fresh Thai fruit instead to end your meal.

A Thai meal is a communal affair: a group of diners will share several dishes, accompanied by steamed white rice. The practical Thais eat with a fork in the left hand and a spoon in the right, using the fork to shovel food onto the spoon and into the mouth.

While hotel restaurants serve some of the city's best food, I've listed on the following pages mostly restaurants outside of hotels. Except in special instances (breakfasts and French *haute cuisine*), you should venture beyond your hotel. The following restaurants are known for their food as much as for their ambience. Note: most Bangkok restaurants close at 10pm; even the majority of hotel coffee shops close at midnight. The price range for dinner for one person, excluding beverage, tax and tips is as follows:
$ = under 250 baht; $$ = 250–350 baht; $$$ = over 350 baht.

Thai

BAAN KHUN LUANG
31/4 Khao Road
Tel: 2410521, 2410928
Located just north of the Krungthon
Bridge, by the riverside, the restaurant
serves Thai, Japanese and Chinese
dishes. One advantage over restaurants
downstream is that it is in a quieter
section of the river, making for a more
tranquil meal. $$

BAAN THAI
7 Soi 32, Sukhumvit Road
Tel: 2585403
Apart from good food, there is the
added bonus of eating in a Thai-style
teak house. Offers a set menu and a
Thai cultural show. $$

BUSSARACUM
39 Pan Road
between Sathorn and Silom
Tel: 2666312
While there is a superb range of curries
(try the *thom kha gai*), the restaurant's
speciality is its appetizers. You can make
an entire meal of them. $$

BENJARONG
Ground floor, Dusit Thani Hotel
Tel: 2360450/9
Superlative royal Thai cuisine served
in exquisite *benjarong* tableware. $$$

CABBAGES & CONDOMS
6-10 Soi 12, Sukhumvit Road
Tel: 2527349
Value-for-money excellent food. If you
are not familiar with Thai food, this
should be one of your first choices.
Profits from this restaurant support
various family planning and HIV aware-
ness programmes. Entertaining gift shop
adjacent. $$

LEMONGRASS
5/1 Soi 24, Sukhumvit Road
Tel: 2588637

This restaurant, actually a large house,
has an intimate feel. The dishes are those
of classic Thai cuisine. $$

PRATUNAM
Petchburi Road
For the adventurous, there are several
open-air restaurants in this area for
dinner, all serving excellent seafood.
Open all night. $

SALA RIM NAAM
Chao Phraya River
opposite the Oriental Hotel
Tel: 4376211, 2360400
The ferry trip from the Oriental across
the river to the restaurant is an excellent
way of starting the evening. The superb
food is complemented by beautiful decor
and a cultural show. $$$

SILOM VILLAGE
286 Silom Road
Tel: 2358760
A complex of small houses and pavilions
with food ordered from the menu or
from vendors. There is an evening Thai
cultural show. $

SPICE MARKET
The Regent Hotel, 155 Ratchadamri
Tel: 2516127
Beautiful ambience, made up to resem-
ble a spice market. Try the daily specials
or the special set menu. $$$

SOI 38
Sukhumvit Road
Best street food, although not every visitor will want to take up this option. Carts and vendors are strung along the *soi* selling noodles, rice, desserts and a dozen other tidbits. Great for sampling a wide variety of the foods ordinary Thais eat. $

THANYING
10 Pramuan Road off Silom Road
Tel: 2364361 and
6th floor, World Trade Centre
Ratchadamri Road
Tel: 2559838
The restaurants serve traditional Thai cuisine. Dinner reservations advisable as the restaurants are frequently crowded. They are a favourite with the local gourmets. $$

WHOLE EARTH
93/3 Soi Lang Suan, Ploenchit Road
Tel: 2525574
The city's only vegetarian Thai restaurant, it serves non-vegetarian food as well for those who can't live without meat. The *yam makua pao*, a roasted eggplant with or without minced shrimp, is delicious. $$

Chinese
SILVER PALACE RESTAURANT
5 Soi Pipat, Silom Road
Tel: 2355118
A wide selection of delicious *dim sum* savouries. $$

Indian
HIMALI CHA CHA
1229/11 Charoen Krung
Tel: 2351569
North Indian menu created by the late Cha Cha, one of Lord Mountbatten's former chefs. $$

RANG MAHAL
Rembrandt Hotel
19 Sukhumvit Soi 18
Tel: 2617100
Serves Northern Indian cuisine to the accompaniment of live Indian music. Great view of the Bangkok skyline. Reservations advised. $$$

Indonesian
BALI
15/3 Soi Ruam Rudee, Ploenchit Rd
Tel: 2543581
Never tried Indonesian food? Then order *Rijstaffel*, a variety of dishes served with rice. $$

This restaurant makes no idle boast of its variety of seafood

Romantic outdoor dining

Vietnamese

LE DALAT
Soi 23, 47/1 Sukhumvit Road
Tel: 2584192
Excellent Vietnamese cuisine, beautifully presented. $$

Japanese

HANAYA
683 Siphya Road
Tel: 2348095
Exemplary service and good ambience. Choose from an excellent range of sushi. $$

Middle Eastern

THE CEDAR
138 Soi 49, Sukhumvit Road
Tel: 3914482
The best of Lebanese food in Bangkok is found here. $$

French

LE NORMANDIE GRILL
The Oriental Hotel
Tel: 2360400, 2360420
Consummate French fare amid elegant surroundings. Designed to resemble the dining car on the Orient Express, the restaurant has a spectacular view of the river. $$$

LE BISTRO
20/18-19 Ruam Rudee Village
Soi Ruam Rudee, Ploenchit Road
Tel: 2529651, 2512523
Fine French dining amid intimate surroundings. There is a wide selection of wines as well. $$$

German

BEI OTTO
1 Sukhumvit Road, Soi 20
Tel: 2620892
It's no exaggeration that you won't find a better German restaurant in Thailand than Bei Otto. $$

English

ANGUS STEAK HOUSE
9/4-5 Thaniya Road
Tel: 2343590
A good range of quality beef dishes. Especially recommended are the steak sandwich and daily specials which are usually excellent. $$

Italian

RISTORANTE SORRENTO
66 North Sathorn Road
Tel: 2349841
Set in an old Neopolitan-style villa, this is one of Bangkok's premier Italian restaurants. $$$

Mexican

EL GORDO'S
130/9 Silom Road, Soi 8
Tel: 234570, 2371415
Apart from the great Mexican food, there is also the live music – a nightly attraction. You can also order icy-cold margaritas by the pitcher. $$

International

THE BARBICAN
9/4-5 Soi Thaniya, Silom
Tel: 2343590
There are salads, stews and more fancier options in this attractive London-style pub. $$

THE TYCOON
118/29-32 Sukhumvit Road, Soi 23
Tel: 6622497
Cosmopolitan food, generous portions, plus private Asian sculpture collection. $$

Nightlife

For many years, Thailand has been regarded as a centre for sex of every persuasion. While its reputation is not altogether undeserved, times and clienteles have somewhat changed. While there has been no decrease in the number of go-go bars and massage parlours, there has been an increase in other activities to meet the needs of the new breed of safe-sex travellers. Jazz clubs, discotheques, pubs and restaurants have proliferated in recent years and are fast becoming the most popular places of entertainment for Thais and tourists alike.

The Thai government, too, tired of the country's image as a sex destination, is taking steps to reduce this unsavoury aspect of the country. In an effort to stem the tide of child prostitution – Thailand has long been a hot-bed for foreign paedophiles – new anti-prostitution laws have been passed, making sex with a minor under the age of 15 a punishable offence.

The infamous Patpong area, which once used to be a hell-raiser's haunt with bargirls and booze, and rough-and-tumble males from around the world, is slowly undergoing changes. The street now boasts numerous restaurants and fast food outlets, discotheques and a pharmacy. Down the centre of the street is a thriving night market which is a good place for visitors to shop for gifts: vendors sell clothes, fake watches, and tourist trinkets. When one overhears a matronly female tourist telling another about the great shopping in Patpong, you know that the street is not what it once was.

Go-Go Bars

There are dozens of naughty bars around and some may find it worthwhile to have a beer and watch the proceedings with an amused air. Bars with hostesses are found at **Nana Entertainment Plaza** (Soi 4, Sukhumvit Rd) and the **Soi Cowboy** (between Sois 21 and 23, Sukhumvit) and **Patpong** (between Silom and Surawong roads) districts. Of the three, Patpong, which is made up of three short streets, is the most well-known: the first two are a welter of neon lights and go-go bars. Patpong

A typical Patpong go-go bar scene

3, like the nearby Silom-Surawong area, caters to an almost exclusively gay crowd.

On Patpong 1, **King's Castle** (the King group reigns supreme on Patpong) is typical. Bikinied go-go girls dance on a platform while others sit on the laps of men quite prepared to shell out a week's salary (and many do) on drinks to keep the young ladies' attentions. Elsewhere there is Thai boxing, and snooker.

The women can be taken out but if it is before the bar closes at 2am, the customer must pay the bar a fee. Other negotiations are entirely between the woman and the customer, with the former very much having the upper hand. Remember, it is a seller's market.

Most first-class hotels are edgy about letting bargirls into the hotel, primarily for security reasons, as the girls occasionally walk away with watches and cash. Most hotels require that the girl leave her ID card with the reception desk overnight. Similarly, with AIDS on the rise, don't take risks; the pharmacy is just down the street.

Live Shows

The live shows at **Supergirls**, **Firecat**, **Pussy Galore** and **Pink Panther** give new definition – not necessarily complimentary – to the word erotic. If you act on the invitations of Patpong touts for 'upstairs' shows, beware of over-pricing and don't go alone. For a nicer atmosphere, **Hollywood 2** and **Rainbow II** at **Nana Plaza** offer pretty girls in safer surroundings.

Beware of live-sex shows off Patpong or along Patpong 2 (the kind the touts want to steer you to). Customers may find themselves being handed extortionate bills of up to 3,000 baht by very large bouncers. If this should happen to you, hand over the money and try to get a copy of the bill. The Tourism Authority operates a 24-hour **Tourist Service Center** information and police emergency hotline: call 1155 for English-speaking help for tourists in trouble. You may also find Tourist Police patrolling the Silom Road end of Patpong. A police kiosk is at the Suriwong Road end of Patpong 2.

Barbeers

Less threatening are the 'barbeers', open-air bars at the end of **Patpong 2**. Here, the primary activity is watching video movies and chatting. **Soi Cowboy** was once regarded as Patpong's poor relative, but in recent years, a numbers of its bars have spiffed themselves up. This street runs between Soi 21 and Soi 23, north of Sukhumvit Road. **Nana Entertainment Complex**, about 80m (260ft) inside Soi 4, Sukhumvit Road, is a warren of 'barbeers', restaurants and nightclubs. The atmosphere is slightly less commercial than Patpong.

Massage Parlours

In massage parlours, the emphasis is upon total relaxation but not achieved in a manner of which mother would approve. Customers pick a woman from behind a glass partition and then spend the next hour getting a bath and whatever else they arrange.

Pubs and Jazz Clubs

Somewhat up-market and nice enough to take a date to are the pubs along **Sukhumvit, Soi 33**. The hostesses here serve and chat, not giggle and cadge drinks, and most speak good English. The pub interiors are well-appointed, the atmosphere is convivial, and the emphasis is upon relaxing after a hard day. They appeal to Thai and foreign professionals and are generally busiest immediately after 5pm. Many pubs bear names of French Impressionist painters, like Vincent Van Gogh, and Monet; **Renoir** is one of the more popular ones.

For a simple evening of good fun and music, try the pubs along **Soi Sarasin**, **Soi Lang Suan** and elsewhere. They differ from their murky, hostess-filled counterparts in being open – usually glass-fronted and with pavement tables.

The emphasis here is on good live music and good conversation. Among the most popular of such pubs you can find are **Brown Sugar** (Soi Sarasin) and **Round Midnight** (Soi Lang Suan). Musicians

All that Jazz at Bobby's Arms

at the **Saxophone** at the Victory Monument (3/8 Phya Thai Rd) play jazz standards. If you like Dixieland jazz and a lively atmosphere, head for **Bobby's Arms** at 8.30 on Sunday evenings. The band comprises local residents who play, and very well too, for the fun of it. Bobby's offers good British cuisine and a wide range of beers in a convivial setting. It is located on the first floor of the carpark next to Foodland on Patpong 2 Road. Billing itself as a Victorian pub, **Witch's Tavern** offers jazz and English roasts at Sukhumvit 55, opposite Soi 9. **Planet Hollywood** at Gaysorn Plaza, and the **Hard Rock Café** in Siam Square, offer music and food in a happy mix. **The Colonade** at the Sukhothai Hotel is also fast becoming a favourite. The **Foreign Correspondents Club of Thailand**, Maneeya Building penthouse, 518/8 Ploenchit Road, welcomes guests to its various programmes and Friday night jazz.

Revitalised **Royal City Avenue** (locals call it RCA) is filled with trendy pubs and restaurants, and even **Disco Bowling**. After 9pm, this modern Brunswick bowling arcade converts to disco with coloured lights, lasers, pounding music and glow-in-the-dark bowling balls. Definitely different!

Several of the more sophisticated, and established, nightclubs are found in first-class hotels. Classy and classic, the Oriental Hotel's famed **Bamboo Bar** is for dressier occasions. The scene is chic, usually with jazz singers from the US playing long-term engagements. You will also find foreign acts at the Dusit Thani Hotel's **Tiara Lounge**.

Discotheques

Patpong has its fair share of discos, many of which continue to throb long after the bars are closed for the night. **Radio City** gets the most attention these days, together with **Lucifers**, complete with glowing masks, giving it mildly satanic ambience. **Rome Club** on Patpong 3 is a gay bar and becomes a discotheque about 9pm. Another hot spot is **Rachadapisek Road**, appealing to Thai party-goers. **Phuture**, near the Chao Phraya Park, and **Sparks**, in the Emerald Hotel, get high marks from locals

The spirited Party House

for both its disco and karaoke. **Spassos** at the Grand Hyatt Erawan Hotel is a perennial favourite, while **Legends** at the Dusit Thani Hotel draws in Thai socialities. **Concept CM2**, Novotel Siam, is a multi-theme nightclub, while **Calypso Cabaret** at the Asia Hotel entertains with its charming transvestites.

Calendar of Special Events

If you are lucky (or a careful planner) your visit will coincide with one of these Thai festivals. The Thais celebrate even their religious holidays with gusto and invite the visitor to join in. As the exact dates for many vary from year to year, check with the Tourism Authority of Thailand.

Kites at Sanam Luang

FEBRUARY – APRIL

Magha Puja: February full-moon night. Celebrates the historical gathering of 1,200 disciples to hear the Buddha preach. In the evening, Buddhists gather at temples to honour him. The most beautiful ceremony is at Wat Benchamabophit (the Marble Wat). Arrive about 7.30pm, and buy incense sticks, a candle and flowers from a vendor. After the sermon, follow the monk-led procession around the temple. After three circuits, place your candle, incense sticks and flowers in the sand-filled trays as others are doing, do a *wai* (hands clasped in prayer before the face) and depart.

Kite-flying Season: Go to Sanam Luang and be a kid again. Buy a snake kite and add it to the thousands of others decorating the skies. Vendors at Chatuchak Park and Lumpini Park also sell kites. On March and April afternoons at 4pm, teams launch huge *chula* kites to battle small *pakpao* kites, each trying to pull the other out of the sky. The coordination and teamwork is fascinating. In the northwest corner are *takraw* competitions, in which teams vie to kick a rattan ball into a basket high overhead.

Songkran: April 12–14. The traditional Thai new year finds the Thais at their boisterous best. On the afternoon of 12 April, Thailand's second most famous Buddha image, the Phra Buddha Sihing, is carried aloft in a solemn procession through the streets to Sanam Luang, where it is anointed by Buddhist devotees. On the following day, 13 April, the Thais bless their friends by sprinkling wa-

Kite in the sky

ter on them, but it soon gets out of hand and water flies everywhere. Bangkok is rather subdued compared with the provinces, but if you wander into Sanam Luang or take a boat up the canals, you are guaranteed at least a dozen dousings. Phrapadaeng, down the Thonburi side of the river, celebrates in more rowdy fashion from 14–16 April.

MAY– JULY

Ploughing Ceremony: Early May. Marks the official beginning of the rice planting season. Presided over by the King, this beautiful, semi-mystical rite predicts the amount of rainfall in the coming monsoon season. Sacred bulls are offered a variety of grains and Brahmin seers note which ones they eat. Obtain tickets beforehand at the TAT office at Bamrung Muang Road. Begins at 7am.

Visakha Puja: May full moon. Commemorates Buddha's birth, enlightenment and death, all of which occurred on the same day. Celebrated in the same manner as Magha Puja.

Asalaha Puja: July full moon. Commemorates Buddha's first sermon to his first five disciples. It is celebrated in the same manner as Magha Puja.

SEPTEMBER – OCTOBER

Chinese Moon Festival: Full moon night of the eighth lunar month. The Chinese celebrate the event by placing small shrines laden with fruit, incense and candles in front of their homes to honour the moon goddess. It is a lovely festival, highlighted by the eating of scrumptious cakes shaped like full moons. Found at no other time of the year, mooncakes are filled with a paste made of either red bean or lotus seed, with a salted egg yolk in the middle.

International Swan Boat Races: Mid-September. Takes place under the Rama 9 Bridge, with participants from around the world.

Chinese Vegetarian Festival: October 7–16. Unlike a similar festival that takes place in Phuket, where penitents pierce their cheeks with iron rods and walk across fire, Bangkok's Vegetarian Festival concentrates on the less gruesome rituals. Every night, in Chinese temples along Sampeng Lane, there are Chinese opera shows, carnival rides, giant incense sticks, and heaps of vegetarian food and delicious sweets found at no other time of the year.

Most Chinese restaurants serve delicious vegetarian dishes at this time. If you dress completely in white clothes, you will be allowed into the inner sanctum of a temple.

NOVEMBER – DECEMBER

Loy Krathong: November full moon. This is the most beautiful of Thai celebrations. On the full moon night, Thais fill tiny boats with candles and incense and launch them into rivers, canals and ponds to wash away sins and bless love affairs.

It is a romantic night better observed on the banks of the Chao Phraya than by a hotel swimming pool. Stand on any of the bridges or at temples like Wat Rakang. If you wish, buy a *krathong* from a vendor. Light the taper and incense, put in a small coin and a few hairs plucked from your head, say a prayer and send it on its way downstream.

Trooping of the Colours: December 3. Two days before his birthday, the King reviews his colourful regiments in a splendid ceremony at the Rama V Plaza. One thousand seats are reserved for tourists on a first-come, first-served basis. Begins at 3pm.

Practical Information

Getting There

Bangkok is served by more than 50 airlines and is a major transportation hub for Southeast Asia. Several airlines fly direct from destinations in Australiasia, Europe and the west coast of the United States. Flying time is about 12 hours from the UK, 19 hours from the west coast of the US and about 9 hours from New Zealand. The domestic arm of Thai Airways operates flights to over 20 other destinations within Thailand, with daily service to tourist hubs like Phuket and Chiang Mai. A 500-baht airport tax is levied for international flights leaving from Bangkok. The tax for domestic flights is 30 baht. For those transfering to an internal flight, a free shuttle bus service connects the international and domestic terminals.

From the Airport

The journey from the airport takes 35 - 100 minutes, depending on the traffic. Two new elevated expressways (20 and 30 baht toll fees) reduce the travel time to most downtown areas to 35 minutes. If you haven't made arrangements with your hotel to pick you up, use one of the following modes of transport:

Cars and taxis: Airconditioned airport limousines are comfortable and convenient, costing between 400 and 600 baht per car. The office is inside the Arrival Hall.

A new and efficient metered public taxi service just outside the Arrival Hall is a cheaper option and just as comfortable. Passengers pay an additional 50 baht on top of the regular taxi fare, as well as expressway toll fees. Non-metered taxis at cheaper set fares are also available, but the cars used may be of a slightly lower standard.

Bus: Public buses are too much of a hassle. Special airport buses go to many downtown destinations for 70 baht. Catch them outside the Arrival Hall.

By Rail

There is a daily link on comfortable, if somewhat slow, trains between Singapore and Bangkok via Butterworth in Malaysia. The same route is also covered by the Eastern & Oriental Express, which offers a nostalgic, if very expensive, travel experience.

For more information, call E&O in Bangkok, tel: 2168661; Singapore, tel: (65) 3923500; London, tel: (0171)

8055100; Germany, tel: (0211) 162106/7; USA, tel: (800) 5242420.

By Road

It is possible to travel by road from Malaysia, either by taxi or tour buses which serve Singapore and Malaysia with Hat Yai in south Thailand. The opening of the Friendship Bridge linking Laos and Nong Khai in 1994 has made road crossings between Laos and Thailand possible.

TRAVEL ESSENTIALS

When to Visit

While Bangkok has a tropical climate, ie hot and humid, there are slight variations in temperature. The best time for a visit is the cool season from mid-November to mid-February.

Visas and Passports

Visitors from many countries, including the UK and US, are issued 30-day entry permits, free, on arrival. Tourist visas for 60- and 90-day stays are available outside the country, depending on one's nationality. It is advisable to check with a Thai embassy or consulate in your country before departure.

Tourist visas can usually be extended at the Immigration Division at Soi Suan Plu, tel: 287-3101 (Monday to Friday, 8.30am to 4pm and Saturdays from 8.30am to 12.30am), before the visa's expiration date. The 30-day entry permits can usually be extended, for a fee of 500 baht, for up to 10 days.

Customs

The import of drugs, dangerous chemicals, pornography, firearms and ammunition is banned. Smuggling heroin and other hard drugs is an offence punishable by death.

Bangkok airport has green and red lanes; searches are usually brief and polite. Foreigners are allowed to import, without tax, one camera with five rolls of film, 200 cigarettes and one litre wine or spirits. There are no limits on the amount of foreign currency a visitor can bring in. On leaving Thailand, the maximum amount of Thai currency that can be taken out without written authorisation is 50,000 baht.

Vaccinations

Cholera, malaria, polio and typhoid vaccinations are recommended for a visit to rural Thailand. A yellow fever vaccination is essential if arriving from an infected country.

Clothing

The heat and humidity makes you hot and sticky very quickly, making the desire to shower twice a day almost obsessive. Clothes should be light and loose; natural fibres or blends that breathe are preferable to synthetics. Sunglasses are essential.

Take note that shorts are taboo for both men and women at Bangkok's major temples; visitors have been turned away by guards for both shabby and casual attire. Shoes must be removed upon entering temple buildings, so slip-ons are best.

Climate

Bangkok's high temperatures and humidity have earned it the World Meteorological Organization's designation as the world's hottest city, an honour arrived at by adding together the daytime highs and the night lows. The seasons are as follows:

Hot season: March to mid-June 27°–35°C (80°–95°F).

Rainy season: June to October 24°–32°C (75°–90°F)

Cool season: November to February 18°–32°C (65°–90°F).

Night temperatures are only slightly lower (sometimes as little as 4°C difference) than daytime and the humidity runs from 70 percent upwards.

The city's salvation is air-conditioning, which chills most hotels, shopping centres and restaurants to almost freezing point. If Bangkok could find a way to air-condition the streets, it would do so, regardless of the cost. Air-conditioned vehicles are especially welcome because Bangkok is not a city for walkers, at least not for distances of more than half a kilometre. An ancillary benefit of air-conditioning is that it filters out the badly polluted air.

Electricity

Electrical outlets are rated at 220 volts, 50 cycles, and accept either flat-pronged or round-pronged plugs.

Time Differences

Thailand is 7 hours ahead of GMT.

GETTING ACQUAINTED

Geography

Thailand, with a population of 60 million people, covers 514,000 sq km, approximately the size of France. Nearly 80 percent of its population is engaged in growing rice, maize, sugar, tapioca and a wide variety of fruits and vegetables. Thailand also has the world's seventh-largest fishing fleet.

Bangkok, the nation's capital, is divided by the Chao Phraya River into twin cities – Bangkok and Thonburi – governed by the same municipality. Situated at 14°N latitude, its 1,565-sq km area (604-sq mile) holds some 8 million people, almost a third of whom are workers registered in up-country villages but living most of time in Bangkok.

Government and Economy

Thailand is a constitutional monarchy with power vested in a freely-elected parliament and a senate appointed by the king from civilian and military officials. The executive branch comprises a coalition of political parties and a prime minister, who in turn rules through a cabinet. There is an independent judiciary.

Thailand enjoys a vigorous free-enterprise economy. Tourism is the principal foreign exchange earner, followed by argicultural produce and commodities. In the late 1980s, Thailand embarked on an ambitious programme of industralisation which has transformed the countryside and recorded annual GNP growth rates as high as 13 percent. It has a well-developed telecommunications, transport and electricity infrastructure. But with rapid growth, all these basic services are now under considerable pressure. Bangkok's congested roads are testimony of this. Thailand's economy took a sharp downtown in mid-1997 and the country is now fighting its way back to recovery.

Religion

About 92 percent of the population are Theravada Buddhists. Five percent are Muslims, most of whom inhabit the south, while the rest comprise Christians, Hindus and Sikhs. The hill tribes practice animism, but many, like the Karen and Lahu, have converted to Christianity.

Population

About 75 percent of Thailand's 60 million population are ethnic Thai. The Chinese, who comprise 12 to 15 percent of the population, represent the largest ethnic minority in the country. Thai Malays of the south make up about 2 percent of the people, and the tribal groups of the northern hills another 1 percent.

How Not to Offend

Thailand's royal family is regarded with genuine reverence by virtually all Thais, and Thais react strongly to ill-considered remarks or the refusal to stand for the royal anthem, such as before the start of every movie; if you fail to stand, you will be told to do so.

Similarly, disrespect towards Buddha images, temples or monks is not taken lightly. Monks are not allowed to touch women, and so when in the vicinity of a monk, a woman should keep her distance to avoid accidentally brushing against him.

The Thai greeting and farewell is *sawasdee*, spoken while raising the hands in a prayer-like gesture, the fin-

gertips touching the nose, and bowing the head slightly. It is reserved for superiors, elders, officials, monks and those who deserve thanks. If in doubt, *wai* anyway. An easy greeting to master, it will earn you smiles wherever you go.

The Thais firmly believe in personal cleanliness and hygiene. They dress, if not richly, at least cleanly and neatly. Unkempt people are frowned upon, as it suggests a lack of self respect and respect for the Thais.

A few other things to note: It is insulting to touch another person on the head (a sacred part of the body), point your feet at him or even step over him, such as when seated. Kicking in anger is worse than spitting at him. In fact, Thais regard displays of anger as a sign of low class behaviour.

There are numerous scoundrels in Bangkok; even if there is ample reason to explode, anger resolves nothing. Blow your top and you will discover how quickly an easy-going Thai can become a stone wall.

MONEY MATTERS

Currency

The Thai baht is divided into 100 satangs. Banknote denominations include 1,000 (light green), 500 (purple), 100 (red), 50 (blue), 20 (green) and 10 (brown) baht notes.

There are 10-baht coins (a brass coin encircled by a brass rim), five-baht coins (silver with copper rims), three variations of one-baht coins (silver, only the small-sized will fit in a public telephone), and two types of 50 and 25 satang coins (both brass-colored).

The Thai baht was floated in mid 1997 after being pegged for many years to the US dollar. In mid-1998, the exchange rate was relatively stable at approximately 40 baht to the US dollar. Check the local papers for current exchange rates.

Rates are more favourable for travellers' checks than for cash.

Credit Cards

American Express, Diners Club, MasterCard and Visa are widely accepted at shops and restaurants throughout Bangkok. Many stores, however, levy a surcharge of between 3 and 5 percent on the use of credit cards, especially American Express cards.

Cash Machines

Visa and Master Card can be used to get cash advances at Bank of Ayutthaya, Thai Farmers Bank, Siam Commercial Bank and the Thai Military Bank. Cash advances for American Express cards can be made at the Bangkok Bank.

Tipping

Most good restaurants, especially those in hotels and elsewhere that cater to foreigners, add a service charge to the bill. However, in ordinary restaurants outside of tourist zones, a tip of 10 to 15 percent will be appreciated.

There is no tipping in noodle shops or for street vendors. Room boys in hotels should be tipped but will not be offended if they are not.

There is no tipping for taxis or *tuk-tuks,* although few drivers will complain if you round up the fare to the next even number.

Thai Banks

BANGKOK BANK
333 Silom Rd
Tel: 2314333

THAI MILITARY BANK
34 Phahonyothin Road
Tel: 2991111

THAI FARMERS BANK
400 Phaholyothin Road
Tel: 2731199

Overseas Banks

BANQUE FRANCAISE DU COMMERCE
Dusit Thani Bldg, 5th floor
946 Rama IV Road
Tel: 2367928

BANK OF TOKYO
Thaniya Bldg
62 Silom Road
Tel: 2369238

CHASE MANHATTAN BANK
North Sathorn Road
Tel: 2345992

CITIBANK
127 Sathorn Thai Road
Tel: 2322000

DEUTSCHE BANK (ASIA)
205 Wireless Road
Tel: 6515000

HONGKONG & SHANGHAI BANK
Hongkong Bank Bldg
64 Silom Road
Tel: 2335995, 2331904

STANDARD CHARTERED BANK
990 Rama IV Road
Tel: 6361000

Credit Card Offices

AMERICAN EXPRESS
388 Paholyothin Road
Tel: 2730044
Open Monday to Friday 8.30am–5.30pm

DINERS CLUB
191 Silom Road
Tel: 2383660 (City-phone 24 hrs)
Open Monday to Friday 8.30am–5pm

MASTERCARD
Sermmit Tower
159 Asoke Road, Sukhumvit 21
Tel: 2608572
Open Monday to Friday 8.30am–5pm

VISA
Sindhorn Bldg Tower 3
15th flr, 130 Wittayu Road
Tel: 2567324/9 (24 hrs)
Open Monday to Friday 8.30am–5pm

GETTING AROUND

Limousines

Major hotels maintain air-conditioned limousines. Although prices are about twice that of taxis, they offer the convenience of English-speaking drivers, door-to-door service and set fares.

Taxis

While Bangkok taxis are air-conditioned, the drivers' command of English is minimal. Metered taxis now dominate and are more comfortable than the old taxis for which fares are bargained. Many metered taxi drivers try and make a fast buck by getting you to agree on a set fare higher than the expected meter fare. Don't step into such a taxi without first agreeing on a price, which can fluctuate depending on the time of day, the amount of traffic the driver has to negotiate, and your destination. In a metered taxi, make sure that the driver switches on the meter at the start of the ride.

The base fare for metered taxis is 35 baht. There is no extra charge for baggage handling and stowage or for extra passengers. Tips are not expected. There are no taxi stands; you stand on the curb and wave down a passing taxi. Avoid parked taxis judiciously, especially outside hotels, as they usually ask more than those you flag down.

Tuk-tuks

Tuk-tuks (also called *samlors*) are the bright blue-and-yellow three-wheeled taxis whose name comes from the noise their two-cycle engines make.

If the English fluency of taxi drivers is limited, that of *tuk-tuk* drivers is even more so. They also like to race and to weave in and out of traffic, providing a hair-raising ride and exposing its occupants to the noxious fumes from Bangkok traffic. Fares begin at 30 baht. *Tuk-tuks* are fun for short trips, but choose a taxi for longer journeys.

Motorcycle Taxis

A good way to negotiate traffic during the rush hour is by motorcyle taxis, found at nearly every intersection. Look for teenage boys wearing colourful vests. The price must be bargained but is usually 10–15 baht for a short distance. Crash helmuts are provided and must be worn, but in case of accidents, forget about collecting insurance.

Buses

Bangkok buses operate every two or three minutes along more than 100 routes and are a good way to see the outer areas of the city. Bus maps give the routes for all types of buses.

Buses are especially useful during rush hours when travelling up one-way streets because they can travel along specially-marked bus lanes going against on-coming traffic. Conductors prowl through the aisles collecting fares and issuing tickets. Unfortunately, destinations are only noted in Thai, so a bus map is needed. Most routes cease operating around midnight, though some (No. 2 and 4) run all through the night.

Ordinary buses come in two varieties: red and white (more expensive) and blue and white. Aside from the price, there is no difference in service routes. Both can be very crowded. It is a sight to see a bus listing heavily to one side while students cling for dear life to the open doors. Green mini-buses are smaller and have less headroom for tall visitors. Their route numbers correspond with those of ordinary buses since they ply the same routes. Air-conditioned executive microbuses (red and blue) hold 40 comfortably seated passengers each at a flat rate of 20 baht. However, these buses serve fewer routes.

Boats

With worsening road traffic conditions in the city, more Bangkok residents are opting to travel by water. There are several options: Chao Phraya white express boats (*rua dan*) travel between Wat Rajingkorn in the south to Nonthaburi in the north, with stops at some 40 piers along the way. Fares range from 4 to 15 baht, depending on the distance, and the waiting time is 15–20 minutes. Express boats with either a triangular red or green flag at the stern do not stop at every pier and charge 1 baht extra for the faster service. Passengers should note that there are few life vests on board these boats and they get very crowded at peak hours.

Commuter long-tail boats (*rua hang yao*), which can seat up to 40 passengers, are designed to negotiate the narrow canals. Routes are fixed and priced according to distance, and the piers are found just adjacent to the express boat piers. Smaller boats, called *rua yon*, which are quieter than the long-tail boats and throw up less spray, are ideal for charter. They seat up to 10 people and can be rented for about 300 baht and up an hour, depending on your ability to bargain.

Elevated Trains

Bangkok's congested traffic is becoming less legendary due to improved management and mass transit. In late 1999 the 24-km (15-mile) line carrying Bangkok Mass Transit Company's elevated trains began serving downtown Bangkok with two intersecting lines, from Mo Chit (Phahol Yothin Road near the Northern

Bus Terminal) to Sukhumvit Soi Onnut in the southeast. Stations include Victory Monument, Siam Square, National Stadium, Chitlom, Nana, Ekamai (Eastern Bus Terminal), Saladaeng-Silom, to Sathorn Road (Taksin Bridge) in the southwest. Construction has begun on an underground line to open in stages beginning in 2002.

Rental Cars

Avis, Hertz and several local agencies offer late-model cars with or without drivers and insurance coverage for Bangkok and up-country trips. An International Driver's Licence is required.

AVIS
2/12 Wireless Road
Tel: 2555300

HIGHWAY CAR RENT
1018/5 Rama IV Road
Tel: 2669393

GRAND CAR RENT
233-5 Soi Asoke
Tel: 2482991/2

HOURS & HOLIDAYS

Business Hours

Business hours are Monday to Friday 8.30am–5.30pm. Some businesses are open Saturdays from 8.30am to noon. Government offices are open Monday to Friday 8.30am–4.30pm.

Banks are open Monday to Friday 8.30am–3.30pm. Many Thai banks operate street money-changing kiosks which are open daily 8.30am–8pm.

Department stores are open daily from approximately 9.30am to 8pm. Ordinary shops open at 8.30 or 9am.

Public Holidays

New Year's Day: January 1
Magha Puja: February full moon
Chakri Day: April 6
Songkran: April 12–14
Labour Day: May 1
Coronation Day: May 5
Visakha Puja: May full moon
Asalaha Puja: July full moon
HM the Queen's Birthday: August 12
Chulalongkorn Day: October 23
HM the King's Birthday: Dec 5
Constitution Day: December 10
New Year's Eve: December 31

Chinese New Year in January or February (the exact dates of the festival are determined by the lunar calendar) is not officially recognised as a holiday, but many shops are closed for four days.

ACCOMMODATION

Bangkok hotels are equal to the very best anywhere in the world. The facilities in the first-class hotels may include as many as six or more different restaurants serving Western and Asian cuisine, coffee shops, swimming pools, exercise rooms, business centres, shopping arcades, and cable and satellite television.

Expect the level of service to be second to none. It is not surprising, therefore, that top Bangkok hotels like the Oriental and the Shangri-La are consistently voted among the best in the world year after year by international business travellers. Even budget and inexpensive hotels will invariably have a swimming pool and more than one food outlet.

Room rates for a double room are categorised as follows: $ = under 1,000 baht; $$ = 1,000–1,999 baht; $$$ = 2,000–2,999 baht; $$$$ = above 3,000 baht. Add another 10 percent service charge and 7 percent VAT to room rates.

AMARI AIRPORT
333 Chert Wudthakas Road
Tel: 5661020/1; Fax: 5661941
Closest hotel to the airport and popular with travellers arriving late and departing early. Connected to airport with footbridge and shuttle bus. $$$$

AMARI BOULEVARD
Soi 7, Sukhumvit Road
Tel: 2552930; Fax: 2552950
A small but luxurious development that many find to be an oasis in a raucous tourist area filled with street markets, noodle shops and bars. $$$$

ARNOMA SWISSOTEL
99 Ratchadamri Road
Tel: 2553410; Fax: 2553456/7
Nice location for business visitors and tourists. Good restaurants and you will enjoy high standards of service. $$$$

BEL-AIRE PRINCESS
16 Soi 5, Sukhumvit Road
Tel: 2534300/30; Fax: 2558850
One of several small 'boutique' hotels offering personalised service and attention. Close to many big business organisations. $$$$

DUSIT THANI
946 Rama IV Road.
Tel: 2360450/9; Fax: 2366400
Bangkok's first highrise hotel. Adjacent to major banks and the business headquarters on Silom Road. Close to nightlife at Patpong. $$$$

EVERGREEN LAUREL
88 North Sathorn Road
Tel: 2667223; Fax: 2667222
Smallish and elegant with a distinct European atmosphere. On a busy thoroughfare but close to big business and foreign embassies. $$$$

GRAND HYATT ERAWAN
494 Ratchadamri Road
Tel: 2541234; Fax: 2535856
On a major intersection and close to the famous Erawan Shrine, one of the best known religious symbols in Bangkok. Just adjacent are major shopping malls. The hotel has a good mix of restaurants and high standards of service. $$$$

HILTON INTERNATIONAL
2 Witthayu Road
Tel: 2530123; Fax: 2536509
Set in beautiful gardens encircling a pool. Close to embassies. Good access to and from the airport. $$$$

HOLIDAY INN CROWNE PLAZA
981 Silom Road
Tel: 2384300; Fax: 2385289
Located between the business centre and the Chao Phraya river. A choice location with small shops nearby. $$$$

IMPERIAL QUEEN'S PARK
36 Soi 22, Sukhumvit Road
Tel: 2619000; Fax: 2619530
With 1,400 rooms, this is Bangkok's biggest hotel. A cavernous place where guests must walk long distances. Interesting shops, bars and restaurants in the vicinity. $$$$

LE MERIDIEN PRESIDENT
135/26 Gaysorn Road
Tel: 2530444, Fax: 2537565
Central location. The hotel has a French flavour and the best hotel coffee shop in town. Elegant shops and restaurants nearby. $$$$

MANSION KEMPINSKI
75/23 Soi 11, Sukhumvit Road
Tel: 2532655; Fax: 2532329
Located in the tourist district, this hotel offers discreet luxury and a hint of central Europe. $$$$

MARRIOT ROYAL GARDEN RIVERSIDE
257/1-3 Charoen Nakhon Road
Tel: 4760022; Fax: 4761120
A resort hotel with the conveniences of nearby downtown. Located on the western side of the river, a bit to the south. The warren of streets nearby offers tourists offbeat glimpses of Bangkok. $$$$

NOVOTEL BANGKOK
Soi 6, Siam Square
Tel: 2556888; Fax: 2361937
A French-managed hotel located in a busy quarter of shops, cinemas, eating places and traffic chaos. $$$$

Entrance to the Grand Hyatt Erawan

ROYAL ORCHID SHERATON
2 Captain Bush Lane, Si Chao Phraya Road. Tel: 2345599; Fax: 2368320
One of the big three riverside hotels (together with the Oriental and the Shangri-La) with incomparable standards of services and exceptional facilities. All are difficult to get to at peak traffic times but guests can travel by river and see little-known areas of Bangkok. $$$$

SHANGRI-LA
89 Soi Wat Suan Plu
Tel: 2367777; Fax: 2368570
Every room has a river view. The evening buffet on the riverside terrace is famous. The biggest hotel on the river. $$$$

SIAM INTERCONTINENTAL
967 Rama 1 Road
Tel: 2530355; Fax: 2532275
With 4 ha (10 acres) of gardens, tennis courts, jogging paths, swimming pools, golf greens and driving ranges this is a cool retreat from the city. Shopping centres, cinemas and restaurants are just beyond the front gates. $$$$

SUKOTHAI BANGKOK
13/3 Sathorn Tai Road
Tel: 2870222; Fax: 2874980
A quiet and luxurious oasis favoured by diplomats. Near the city's centre on a busy thoroughfare but set well back amid tropical gardens. $$$$

THE LANDMARK
138 Sukhumvit Road
Tel: 2540404; Fax: 2534259
Central location, and near airport road. Well-equipped for business travellers and shoppers. $$$$

THE ORIENTAL
48 Oriental Ave
Tel: 2360400/20; Fax: 2361937

A visit is a must, even if it is only to have a drink on the river terrace. The Oriental is part of the history of East meeting West. Repeatedly voted one of the world's best hotels. $$$$

THE PAN PACIFIC
952 Rama IV Road
Tel: 26329000; Fax: 26329001
Plush hotel close to shopping areas, Lumpini Park and the Patpong district. The swimming pool is an oasis of relaxation. $$$$

THE REGENT BANGKOK
155 Ratchadamri Road
Tel: 2516127; Fax: 2539195
High luxury in the heart of the city. With music and tea in the lobby lounge, there are echoes of the old Orient. The best hotel pool in Bangkok. $$$$

AMBASSADOR
171 Soi 1113, Sukhumvit Road
Tel: 2540444; Fax: 2534123
A sprawling complex that offers one of the city's biggest array of Asian and European restaurants. $$$

BANGKOK PALACE
1091/336 New Phetchaburi Road
Tel: 2550305; Fax: 2533359.
A 670-room hotel located near the lively Pratunam Market. $$$

BAIYOKE SUITE
2130 Ratchaprarop Road
Tel: 2550330; Fax: 2545533
Also near Pratunam Market. Dine at the Sky Lounge for a superb view of the city. $$$

INDRA REGENT
120/126 Ratchaprarop Road
Tel: 2521111; Fax: 2533849
Comfortable hotel surrounded by old markets and eating places which are gradually making way for Thailand's largest wholesale centre for garments. $$$

NEW PENINSULA
293/5 Surawongse Road
Tel: 2343910/7; Fax: 2365526
Good value for money, with restaurants,

The incomparable Oriental at dusk

cocktail lounge, swimming pool, but small rooms. 10 minutes from the river. $$$

SOL TWIN TOWERS
88 New Rama VI Road
Tel: 2169555/6; Fax: 2169544
Large international-class 700-room hotel with easy access to the city's tourist and commercial areas. $$$

TAI-PAN
25 Soi 23, Sukhumvit Road
Tel: 2609898; Fax: 2597908
A tasteful hotel in the busy Sukhmvit area. Restaurant and swimming pool. $$$

ARISTON
19 Soi 24, Sukhumvit Road
Tel: 2590960/9; Fax: 2590970
With a 24-hour coffee-shop and swimming pool. $$

Sol Twin Towers is good value for money

EURO INN
Soi 31, Sukhumuit Road
Tel: 2599480; Fax: 2599490
Convenient to shopping and entertainment areas. $$

NEW TROCADERO
34 Surawong Road
Tel: 2348920/9; Fax: 2348929
Popular with Westerners. Good travel services. $$

A ONE INN
1315 Soi Kasemsan 1
Tel: 2164770; Fax: 2164771
Located beside Siam Square and close to World Trade Centre. Spacious rooms and friendly service. $

ATLANTA
78 Soi 2, Sukhumvit Road
Tel: 2521650/6069; Fax: 6568123
Good value for money. Well regarded by return visitors. $

CHINA INN
19/2728 Soi 19, Sukhumvit Road
Tel: 2557571/3; Fax: 2541333 $

EMBASSY
21 Pradipat Road
Tel: 2798441; Fax: 2783600
$

EURASIA BANGKOK
33/2 Soi Wattananivet 7
Sutthisan Road, Ratchadapisek
Tel: 2750060/77; Fax: 2752221
$

MUANGPHOL MANSION
Soi Kasem San 1, Rama 1
Tel: 2150033; Fax: 2168053
$

Guesthouses

If on a limited budget, there are numerous guesthouses offering clean and economical accommodation. Once of primary interest only to backpackers because of their spartan facilities, many have now been upgraded to include fans, air-conditioning and private bathrooms. Generally possessing no more than a dozen rooms, these establishments are run more like pensions than hotels. Prices range from 80 to 250 baht a night. Most guesthouses in Bangkok are found along Khaosarn Road and Soi Ngam Duphli, off Rama IV Road.

HEALTH AND EMERGENCIES
Hygiene

Reserve Bangkok's tap water for bathing and teeth-brushing and drink only bottled water. Most hotels and large restaurants offer bottled water and clean ice; elsewhere, you must request for it. Avoid cold food, salads, and peeled fruits. Thai chefs understand the importance of hygiene in preparing meals, and the chances of becoming ill are minimal.

With its thriving nightlife and transient population, Bangkok is a magnet for venereal diseases; protect yourself. With AIDS on the rise, there is even more reason to be careful.

Hospitals

Bangkok's first-class hotels have doctors on call to treat medical emergencies. For more serious cases, Bangkok has ambulances and hospitals the equivalent of any major Western city. Hospital intensive care units are fully equipped to handle any emergency quickly and competently. Many Thai doctors have trained in Western hospitals, although some may not be very fluent in English.

BANGKOK ADVENTIST HOSPITAL
430 Phitsanuloke Road
Tel: 2811422, 2821100

BANGKOK CHRISTIAN HOSPITAL
124 Silom Road
Tel: 2336981/9, 2351000/7

BANGKOK GENERAL HOSPITAL
2 Soi Soonvijai, New Petchaburi Road
Tel: 3180066, 3181549/52

BNH HOSPITAL
9/1 Convent Road, Silom Road
Tel: 6320550, 6320560

BUMRUMGRAD HOSPITAL
33 Soi 3, Sukhumvit Road
Tel: 2530250

DEJA GENERAL HOSPITAL
346 Sri Ayutthaya
Tel: 2460137, 2461685/93

SAMITIVEJ HOSPITAL
133 Soi 49, Sukhumvit Road
Tel: 3920011, 3816807

SIAM GENERAL HOSPITAL
15/10 Soi Chokchai 4, Lardprao
Tel: 5142157/9, 5142273

Dental Clinics

Dental clinics are as numerous as medical clinics. The **Dental Polyclinic**, at 211-3 New Petchburi Rd, tel: 3145070,
3147177, has a long-standing reputation. Another alternative is the **Dental Hospital** at 88 Soi 49, Sukhmvit Road, tel: 2605000/15. It looks more like a hotel than a dental hospital and has the latest imported equipment.

Snake Bites

The chances of being bitten by a poisonous snake in Bangkok are virtually nil, but should it occur, most hospitals have anti-venom serum on hand. If they don't, go to the **Saowapha Institute** (Snake Farm) at 1871 Rama IV Road.

Pharmacies

Pharmaceuticals are produced to international standards, and most pharmacies have registered pharmacists on premises. Most pharmacy personnel in the shopping and business areas speak English.

Crime

Bangkok is generally free of violent crime. It is necessary, however, to say that behind some of the Thai smiles lurk evil intent. With increased tourist arrivals, pickpockets are on the rise.

When walking in the street, keep your money and credit cards in your front pocket or shirt; clutch your purse tightly in front of you. Many pickpockets carry

A Chinese herbal shop

sharp razors and can slit through a purse and remove a wallet without you knowing it. Ride in the front rather than the back of a bus.

At major tourist attractions, beware of men and women offering you a free tour or to take you to a shop offering special prices, especially on gems you can resell in your country at a profit.

Similarly, at boat docks, avoid men offering you a free ride on canal boats; they'll literally take you for a ride. Walk past bogus Boy Scouts with notebooks soliciting donations; it is a scam. Above all, don't succumb to the lure of easy money by getting into a card game; it is rigged against your winning.

Finally, beware touts on Patpong offering 'upstairs' live sex shows. Once inside, one is handed an exorbitant bill and threatened with mayhem if he or she protests. Pay, take the receipt, and report immediately to the Tourist Police. Call 1155 and go personally to the police (see below) for possible restitution.

Police Emergencies

In Bangkok, the police emergency number, in Thai, is 191; in English, 1155. Tourist Police can be contacted at TPI Tower, Chantatmai Road, tel: 6786800/9 or at Tourist Service Centre, TAT, Ratchadamnoen Road, tel: 1155. Tourist police are at sites like the Grand Palace and most speak some English.

COMMUNICATIONS AND NEWS

Post & Telecommunications

Post offices are open from 8.30am to 4pm and later depending on location. The General Post Office in Charoen Krung, not far from the Oriental Hotel, opens from Monday to Friday 7.30am–4.30pm; Saturday and Sunday 9am–noon. In addition to the postal service, Bangkok offers a number of international courier agencies including Federal Ex-

press, DHL and TNT Skypak.

Most hotels have long-distance telephones, telegrams, mail, telex and fax facilities. To call abroad directly, first dial the international access code 001, followed by the country code: Australia (61); France (33); Germany (49); Italy (39); Japan (81); Netherlands (31); Spain

(34); UK (44); US and Canada (1). If using a US credit phone card, dial the company's access number, followed by 01, then the country code. Sprint, tel: 001 999 13 877; AT&T, tel: 0019 991 1111; MCI, tel: 001 999 1 2001.

To call Bangkok from overseas, dial the country code 66, followed by Bangkok's area code 2. Long distance calls can also be placed from the General Post Office annex on the ground floor of the Nava Building in Soi Braisanee, just north of the GPO. Open 24 hours.

Shipping

Most shops handle documentation and shipping for your purchases. Alternatively, the General Post Office in Charoen Krung offers boxes and a packing service for goods being sent by sea mail.

Media

The Bangkok Post and The Nation are among the best and most comprehensive English-language dailies in Asia. The Asian Wall Street Journal and the International Herald Tribune and editions of British, French, German and Italian newspapers are available at hotel newsstands of major hotels.

FM radio has several stations playing the latest pop hits and oldies. English-language news and popular music can be heard on 95.5 FM and 105.5 FM. These stations also broadcast news and travel programmes that are made by Radio Thailand.

Bangkok has five Thai language television channels. In addition, there is cable television network ITV and Thai Sky satellite TV. Most major hotels and many smaller ones carry a wide selection of television channels and services.

USEFUL INFORMATION

Maps

Apart from the included pull-out map in this guide, Nancy Chandler's Market Map has been a good standby for years because of its colourful, detailed maps of Bangkok's major markets. The Jim Thompson House sells old maps of Siam, which, when framed, make handsome home decor items.

Export Permits for Antiques

The Fine Arts Department prohibits the export of all Buddha images, images of other deities and fragments (hand or heads) of images created before the 18th century.

All antiques and art objects, regardless of type or age, must be registered with the Fine Arts Department. The shop where you made your purchase will usually do this for you.

If you decide to handle it yourself, take the piece to the Fine Arts Department on Na Prathat Road across from Sanam Luang, together with two postcard-sized photos of it. The export fee is between 50 and 200 baht, depending on the age of the item.

Take note that fake antiques do not require export permits. However, airport customs officials are not art experts and they may mistake one for a genuine piece; so do not take chances, if it looks authentic, clear it first at the Fine Arts Department to avoid any problems.

Children

Children enjoy the unusual animals of **Dusit Zoo**, or paddling boats in its lake or in **Lumpini** or **Chatuchak parks**.

Magic Land at 72 Paholyothin Road, near the Central Plaza Hotel, is an amusement park with a ghost house, bumper cars and carnival rides.

On weekdays, the ticket covers an unlimited number of rides. On weekends, the ticket is limited to two hours. Open 10am–5.30pm Monday to Friday; 9.30am–7pm Saturday and Sunday.

East of town at 101 Sukhapiban 2 Road is **Siam Park City**, a theme park with water slides and flumes. It is open 10am–6pm, Monday to Friday; and 9am–7pm, Saturday and Sunday.

A word of warning: the park prohibits the wearing of T-shirts in the swimming areas so take plenty of suntan oil for tender young skins.

Safari World is an amusement park that children will find fascinating. Located about 10 km (6¼ miles) from the centre of town, it can be reached by minibus.

Disabled

Facilities for the handicapped are underdeveloped. Sidewalks are uneven, studded with obstructions and there are no ramps. Few buildings in Bangkok have wheelchair ramps.

Bookshops

There are several excellent book stores in Bangkok. **DK Bookhouse** in Siam Square and **Asia Books** with branches in Sukhumvit Road between Sois 17 and 19, the Landmark Hotel, World Trade Center, and the Peninsula Plaza all carry a wide variety of books related to Thailand.

LANGUAGE

Origins and Intonation

For centuries, the Thai language, rather than tripping from foreigners' tongues, has been tripping them up. Its roots go back to the place Thais originated from, in the hills of southern Asia but overlaid by Indian influences.

From the original settlers come the five tones which seem designed to frustrate visitors – one sound with five different tones to mean five different things.

When you mispronounce, you don't simply say a word incorrectly, you say another word entirely. It is not unusual to see a semi-fluent foreigner standing before a Thai running through the scale of tones until suddenly a light of recognition dawns on his companion's face.

There are misinformed visitors who will tell you that tones are not important. These people do not communicate with Thais, they communicate at them in a one-sided exchange that frustrates both parties.

Thai Names

From the languages of India have come polysyllabic names and words, the lexicon of literature. Thai names are among the longest in the world. Every Thai first and surname has a meaning. Thus, by learning the meaning of the name of everyone you meet, you would acquire a quite extensive vocabulary.

There is no universal transliteration system from Thai into English, which is why names and street names can be spelled three different ways.

For example, the surname Chumsai is written Chumsai, Jumsai and Xoomsai depending on the family. This confuses even the Thais. If you ask a Thai how you spell something, he may well reply 'how do you want to spell it?' Likewise, Bangkok's thoroughfare of Ratchadamnern is also spelt as Rajadamnoen. The spellings will differ from map to map, and book to book.

Phonology

The way Thai consonants are written in English often confuses foreigners. An "h" following a letter like 'p', and 't' gives the letter a soft sound; without the 'h' the sound is more explosive. Thus, 'ph' is not pronounced 'f' but as a soft 'p'. Without the 'h', the 'p' has the sound of a very hard 'b'.

The word Thanon (street) is pronounced 'tanon' in the same way as 'Thailand' is not meant to sound like 'Thighland.' Similarly, final letters are often not pronounced as they look. A 'j' on the end of a word is pronounced 't'; 'l' is pronounced as an 'n'. To complicate matters further, many words end with 'se' or 'r' which are not usually pronounced.

Vowels are pronounced like this: 'i' as in sip, 'ii' as in seep, 'e' as in bet, 'a' as in pun, 'aa' as in pal, 'u' as in pool, 'o' as in so, 'ai' as in pie, 'ow' as in cow, 'aw' as in paw, 'iw' as in you, 'oy' as in toy.

In Thai, the pronoun 'I' and 'me' use the same word but it is different for males and females. Men use the word *phom* when referring to themselves; women say *chan* or *diichan*.

Men use *khrap* at the end of a sentence when addressing either a male or a female i.e. pai (f) *nai, khrap* (h) (where are you going sir?).

Women add the word *kha* to their statements as in *pai* (f) *nai, kha* (h).

To ask a question, you add a high tone *mai* to the end of the phrase ie *rao pai* (we go) or *rao pai mai* (h) (shall we go?).

To negate a statement, insert a falling tone *mai* between the subject and the verb ie *rao pai* (we go), *rao mai pai* (we don't go).

'Very' or 'much' are indicated by adding *maak* to the end of a phrase ie *ron* (hot), *ron maak* (very hot).

Following is a small vocabulary with handy phrases related to numbers, directions and greetings intended to get you on your way.

The five tones have been indicated by appending letters after them viz high (h), low (l), middle (m), rising (like asking a question) (r), and falling (like suddenly understanding something as in 'ohh, I see') (f).

Useful Phrases

Numbers
1/Nung (m)
2/Song (r)
3/Sam (r)
4/Sii (m)
5/Haa (f)
6/Hok (m)
7/Jet (m)
8/Pat (m)
9/Kow (f)
10/Sip (m)
11/Sip Et (m, m)
12/Sip Song (m, r)
13/Sip Sam (m, r) and so on
20/Yii Sip (m, m)
30/Sam Sip (f, m) and so on
100/Nung Roi (m, m)
1,000/Nung Phan (m, m)

Days of the Week
Monday/Wan Jan
Tuesday/Wan Angkan
Wednesday/Wan Phoot
Thursday/Wan Pharuhat
Friday/Wan Sook
Saturday/Wan Sao
Sunday/Wan Athit
Today/Wan nii (h)
Yesterday/Mua wan nii (h)
Tomorrow/Prung nii (h)
When/Mua (f) rai

Greetings and others
Hello, goodbye
Sawasdee (a man then says khrup; a woman says kha; thus sawasdee khrup)
How are you?/Khun sabai dii, mai (h)
Well, thank you/Sabai dii, Khapkhun
Thank you very much/Khapkhun Maak
May I take a photo?
Thai roop (f) noi, dai (f) mai (h)
Never mind/Mai (f) pen rai
I cannot speak Thai
Phuut Thai mai (f) dai (f)
I can speak a little Thai
Phuut Thai dai (f) nit (h) diew
Where do you live?
Khun yoo thii (f) nai (r)
What is this called in Thai?
An nii (h), kaw riak aray phasa Thai
How much?/Thao (f) rai

Directions and Travel
Go/Pai
Come/Maa
Where/Thii (f) nai (r)
Right/Khwaa (r)
Left/Sai (h)
Turn/Leo
Straight ahead/Trong pai
Please slow down/Cha cha noi
Stop here/Yood thii (f) nii (f)
Fast/Raew
Hotel/Rong raam
Street/Thanon
Lane/Soi
Bridge/Saphan
Police Station/Sathanii Dtam Ruat

Other Handy Phrases
Yes/Chai (f)
No/Mai (f) chai (f)
Do you have...?/Mii...mai (h)
Expensive/Phaeng
Do you have something cheaper?
Mii arai thii thook (l) kwa, mai (h)
Can you lower the price a bit?
Kaw lot noi dai (f) mai (h)
Do you have another colour?
Mii sii uhn mai (h)
Too big/Yai kern pai
Too small/Lek kern pai
Do you have bigger?
Mii arai thii yai kwa mai (h)
Do you have smaller?
Mii arai thii lek kwa mai (h)
Hot (heat hot)/Ron (h)
Hot (spicy)/Phet
Cold/Yen
Sweet/Waan (r)
Sour/Prio (f)
Delicious/Aroy
I do not feel well/Mai (f) sabai

Glossary of Temple Terms

Bot: The ordination hall, usually open only to the monks. Some *wat* do not have a *bot*.
Chedi: Often interchangeable with *stupa*. A mound surmounted by a spire in which relics of the Buddha are supposedly kept. Influential families also build small *chedi* to hold the ashes of their forebears.
Chofah: The bird-like decoration on the end of a *bot* or *viharn* roof.
Naga: A serpent, usually running down

the edge of the roof sheltering Buddha as he meditates.

Prang: An Ayutthayan-style *chedi*, looking somewhat like a vertical ear of corn. Wat Arun is a good example.

Sala: An open-sided pavilion.

Viharn: The sermon hall, the busiest building in a *wat*. A temple may have more than one.

Wat: Translated as 'temple', but describing a collection of buildings and monuments within a compound wall.

USEFUL ADDRESSES

Tourist Information

Planning a trip to Thailand can be made easier if you contact a travel agent or an office of the Tourism Authority of Thailand. These offices offer promotional brochures, maps and videotapes of the country's many attractions.

The Tourism Authority of Thailand (TAT) is the Thai government's official tourism promotion organisation. For a complete 24-hour information service phone 1155 or call at its Tourism Service Centre at 4 Ratchadamnoen Nok. Tourists may also call the head office at Le Concorde Plaza, 202 Ratchadapisek Road (tel: 6941222). It has a wealth of brochures on various attractions and personnel to answer questions.

TAT has its own travel information site on the Internet: http://www.tat.or.th. The TAT's e-mail address for inquiries is info1@tat.or.th.

Numerous travel magazines, free at hotels, give current information on events and attractions. *Metro* magazine available in most bookshops, is particularly useful source for events and services.

Airline Offices

AIR FRANCE
20F Vorawat Building
849 Silom Road
Tel: 6351199, 6351200
Airport: 5237302, 5352112-3

AIR INDIA
S.S. Building,
10/12-13 Convent Road, Silom
Tel: 2350557; Airport: 5352122

AIR LANKA
Charn Issara Bldg
942/51 Rama IV Road
Tel: 2360159, 2369292
Airport: 5352331/2

AIR NEW ZEALAND
World Travel Service
1053 Charoen Krung 39
Tel: 2371560; Airport: 5353981

BANGKOK AIRWAYS
Queen Sirikit National Convention Center
New Ratchadapisek Road
Tel: 2293434; Airport: 5352497

BRITISH AIRWAYS
14F Abdulrahim Building
990 Rama IV Road
Tel: 6361747; Airport: 5352220

CANADIAN AIRLINES
6th floor, Maneeya Building
518/5 Ploenchit Road
Tel: 2514521; Airport: 5352227/8

CATHAY PACIFIC
11F Ploenchit Tower, Ploenchit Road
Tel: 2630606; Airport: 5352155

CHINA AIRLINES
4th floor, Peninsula Plaza
153 Ratchadamri Road
Tel: 2534242; Airport: 5355201-4

DELTA AIRLINES
Patpong Building, Suriwong Road
Tel: 2376847-9; Airport: 5352991

GARUDA INDONESIA
27F Lumpini Tower, Rama IV Road
Tel: 2856470; Airport: 5352171

JAPAN AIRLINES
JAL Building, 254/1 Ratchadapisek Road
Tel: 2741411/25; Airport: 5352135

KLM
19F Thai Wah Twr II, South Sathorn
Tel: 6791100; Airport: 5237277

KOREAN AIR
699 Silom Road
Tel: 6350465; Airport: 5352335

LAO AVIATION
491/17 Silom Plaza, Silom Road
Tel: 2369822; Airport: 5353786

LUFTHANSA
18F Q House (Asoke)
66 Sukhumvit Soi 21
Tel: 2642400/8; Airport: 5352213

MALAYSIA AIRLINES
Ploenchit Tower
Ploenchit Road
Tel: 2630565; Airport: 5352288

MYANMAR AIRWAYS
Jewelry Trade Center, Silom Road
Tel: 6300334; Airport: 5352484

PAKISTAN INTERNATIONAL
Chongkolnee Bldg,
56 Surawong Road
Tel: 2335215; Airport: 5352127

QANTAS
14F Abdulrahim Place
990 Rama IV Road
Tel: 6361747; Airport: 5352220

ROYAL AIR CAMBODGE
17F Pacific Place,
142 Sukhumvit Road
Tel: 6532261-6; Airport: 5353679

ROYAL BRUNEI
4th floor, Charn Issara Bldg
942/52 Rama IV Road
Tel: 2330056; Airport: 5352626

SAS
8F Glas Haus Bldg
Sukhumvit Soi 25
Tel: 2600444; Airport: 5338991

SINGAPORE AIRLINES
12th floor, Silom Center Building
2 Silom Road
Tel: 2360440; Airport: 5238268

THAI AIRWAYS
Head office: 89 Vibhadi Rangsit Road,
Tel: 2800060; Silom: 485 Silom Road,
Tel: 2343100; Rajawong: 45 Anuwong
Road, Tel: 2239746/9; Asia Hotel: Tel:
2152020; Airport: 5352278

UNITED AIRLINES
9th floor, Regent House
183 Ratchadamri Road
Tel: 2530558; Airport: 5352241

VIETNAM AIRLINES
Ploenchit Centre,
2-4 Sukhumvit Soi 2
Sukhumvit Road
Tel: 6569058; Airport: 5352671/5327

Embassies

AUSTRALIA
37 Sathorn Tai Road
Tel: 2872680. Visas: 8.15am–12.15pm

AUSTRIA
14 Soi Nantha
Sathorn Tai Road
Tel: 2873970/2. Visas: 9am–noon

BELGIUM
44 Soi Pipat
off Silom Road
Tel: 2367876. Visas: 8.30am–1pm

CAMBODIA
185 Rajdamri Road
Tel: 2546630, 2539851
Visas: Monday–Friday 9–11am

CANADA
15F Abdulrahim Place
990 Rama IV Road
Tel: 6360560; Fax: 6360565

DENMARK
10 Soi Atthakan Prasit
Sathorn Tai Road
Tel: 2132021/5. Visas: 9am–3pm
(Friday: 9am–noon)

FRANCE
29 South Sathorn Road (consular section)
Tel: 2132181/4. Visas: 8.30am–noon

GERMANY
9 Sathorn Tai Road
Tel: 2879000
Visas: 8.30–11.30am

INDIA
46 Sukhumvit Soi 23 (Soi Prasanmit)
Sukhumvit Road.

Tel: 2580300-6
Visas: 9am–noon

INDONESIA
600-602 New Phetchaburi Road
Tel: 2523135/39
Visas: 8.30am–noon and 1.30–3.30pm

ITALY
399 Nang Linchi Road
Tung Mahamek
Tel: 2854090. Visas: 9.30–11.30am

JAPAN
9F Sermmit Tower
159 Sukhumvit Soi 21
Tel: 2590725, 2590444, 2589915.
Visas: Monday–Friday 8.30am–noon

LAOS
502/1-2 Ramkhamhaeng Soi 39
Bangkapi
Tel: 5383696. Visas: 8am–noon

MALAYSIA
15F Regent House
183 Ratchadamn
Tel: 2541700. Visas: 8.30–11.30am

MYANMAR
132 Sathorn Nua Road
Tel: 2332237, 2344698.
Visas: 8.30am–noon

NEPAL
189 Sukhumvit Soi 71, Phrakanong
Tel: 3917240. Visas: 9am–noon

NETHERLANDS
106 Witthayu Road
Tel: 2547701/5. Visas: 9am–noon

NEW ZEALAND
93 Witthayu Road
Tel: 2542530. Visas: 8.30–11.30am

SINGAPORE
129 Sathorn Tai Road
Tel: 2862111, 2861434
Visas: 8.30am–noon

SWITZERLAND
35 Witthayu Road
Tel: 2530156/60. Visas: 9am–noon

UNITED KINGDOM
1031 Ploenchit Road
Tel: 2530191/9
Visas: 8–11am (Friday: 8am–noon)

UNITED STATES
95 Wittayu Road (consular section)
Tel 2054000. Visas: 7–10am

VIETNAM
83/1 Wittayu Road
Tel: 2515835, 2517202
Visas: Monday–Saturday 8.30–11.30am

FURTHER READING
History

Lords of Life by Chakrabongse, Prince
Chula, Alvin Redman, London, 1960.
A history of the Chakri Kings.
Mongkut, the King of Siam by Moffat,
Abbot Low, Ithaca, New York: Cornell
University Press, 1961. Superb history
of one of Asia's most interesting 19th
century men.
The Thai Peoples by Seidenfaden, Erik,
Siam Society, Bangkok, 1967. Solid
work by a long-time resident.
The Arts of Thailand by Van Beek, Steve,
Travel Publishing Asia, Hong Kong,
1985. Lavishly illustrated, includes the
minor arts.
The House on the Klong by Warren,
William, Tokyo, Weatherhill. The story
of the Jim Thompson House.
Culture Shock: Thailand by Cooper,
Robert and Nanthapa, Times Books, Sin-
gapore, 1982. Useful and funny look at
Thai customs.
Mai Pen Rai by Hollinger, Carol,
Hougthon Mifflin, Boston. Expatriate
life in the 1950s.
Essays on Thai Folklore by Rajadhon,
Phya Anuman, Bangkok, DK Books. A
description of Thai ceremonies, festivals
and rites of passage.
*The Balancing Act: A History of Modern
Thailand* by Joseph Wright, Oakland:
Pacific Rim Press, 1991.
Insight Guide: Bangkok by Van Beek,
Steve and others, Apa Publications, Sin-
gapore, 2000.

Index

ACKNOWLEDGMENTS

Photography	Ingo Jezierski *and*
12, 16, 17, 23, 32, 33, 36, 39T, 40, 50T, 51, 52, 53B, 61, 64, 65, 69, 75, 76, 79, 80, 82, 83, 84	Marcus W Smith
39B, 46, 72, 78	Francis Dorai
11, 55T, 63	Luca Invernizzi Tettoni
61B	Hans Höfer
81	Courtesy of Sol Twin Towers
Update Editor	Sandy Barron
Desktop Operators	Caroline Low
Handwriting	V Barl
Cover Design	Klaus Geisler
Cartography	Berndtson & Berndtson

NOTES

The World o

400 books in three complementary serie

nsight Guides

●ver every major destination in every continent.

Bhutan★
Boston★
British Columbia★
Brittany★
Brussels★
Budapest &
  Surroundings★
Canton★
Chiang Mai★
Chicago★
Corsica★
Costa Blanca★
Costa Brava★
Costa del
Sol/Marbella★
Costa Rica★
Crete★
Denmark★
Fiji★
Florence★
Florida★
Florida Keys★
French Riviera★
Gran Canaria★
Hawaii★
Hong Kong★
Hungary
Ibiza★
Ireland★
Ireland's Southwest★
Israel★
Istanbul★
Jakarta★
Jamaica★
Kathmandu *Bikes &*
  Hikes★
Kenya★
Kuala Lumpur★
Lisbon★
Loire Valley★
London★
Macau
Madrid★
Malacca
Maldives
Mallorca★
Malta★
Mexico City★
Miami★
Milan★
Montreal★
Morocco★
Moscow
Munich★

Nepal★
New Delhi
New Orleans★
New York City★
New Zealand★
Northern California★
Oslo/Bergen★
Paris★
Penang★
Phuket★
Prague★
Provence★
Puerto Rico★
Quebec★
Rhodes★
Rome★
Sabah★
St Petersburg★
San Francisco★
Sardinia
Scotland★
Seville★
Seychelles★
Sicily★
Sikkim
Singapore★
Southeast England
Southern California★
Southern Spain★
Sri Lanka★
Sydney★
Tenerife★
Thailand★
Tibet★
Toronto★
Tunisia★
Turkish Coast★
Tuscany★
Venice★
Vienna★
Vietnam★
Yogyakarta
Yucatan Peninsula★

**★ = *Insight Pocket
Guides*
with Pull out Maps**

Insight Compact Guides

Algarve
Amsterdam
Bahamas
Bali
Bangkok

Barbados
Barcelona
Beijing
Belgium
Berlin
Brittany
Brussels
Budapest
Burgundy
Copenhagen
Costa Brava
Costa Rica
Crete
Cyprus
Czech Republic
Denmark
Dominican Republic
Dublin
Egypt
Finland
Florence
Gran Canaria
Greece
Holland
Hong Kong
Ireland
Israel
Italian Lakes
Italian Riviera
Jamaica
Jerusalem
Lisbon
Madeira
Mallorca
Malta
Milan
Moscow
Munich
Normandy
Norway
Paris
Poland
Portugal
Prague
Provence
Rhodes
Rome
St Petersburg
Salzburg
Singapore
Switzerland
Sydney
Tenerife
Thailand

Turkey
Turkish Coast
Tuscany
UK regional titles:
  Bath & Surroundings
  Cambridge & East
    Anglia
  Cornwall
  Cotswolds
  Devon & Exmoor
  Edinburgh
  Lake District
  London
  New Forest
  North York Moors
  Northumbria
  Oxford
  Peak District
  Scotland
  Scottish Highlands
  Shakespeare Country
  Snowdonia
  South Downs
  York
  Yorkshire Dales
USA regional titles:
  Boston
  Cape Cod
  Chicago
  Florida
  Florida Keys
  Hawaii: Maui
  Hawaii: Oahu
  Las Vegas
  Los Angeles
  Martha's Vineyard &
    Nantucket
  New York
  San Francisco
  Washington D.C.
Venice
Vienna
West of Ireland